CHICAGO PUBLIC LIBRARY
HAROLD WASHINGTON LIBRARY CENTER

R0013243772

REF
LB   Davis, Jerry S.
2337.4
.D38   Guide to the
          literature of
          student financial
          aid

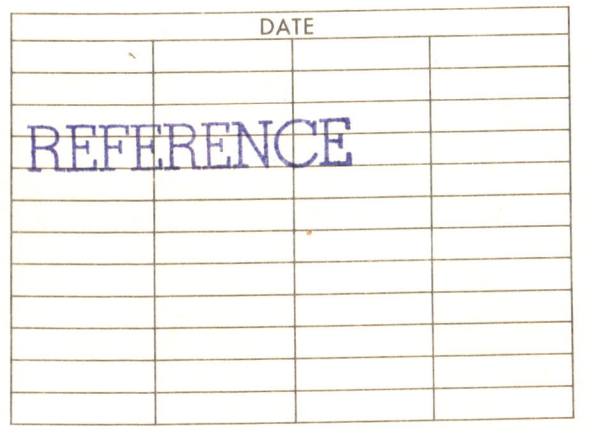

cop. 1   FORM 125 M

SOCIAL SCIENCES AND HISTORY DIVISION

The Chicago Public Library

MAR - 8 1980

Received

© THE BAKER & TAYLOR CO

Guide to the Literature of Student Financial Aid

Jerry S. Davis and William D. Van Dusen

College Entrance Examination Board, New York, 1978

REF
LB
2337.4
.D38   cop. 1

Copies of this book may be ordered from College Board Publication Orders, Box 2815, Princeton, New Jersey 08541. The price is $7.

Editorial inquiries concerning this book should be directed to Editorial Office, The College Board, 888 Seventh Avenue, New York, New York 10019.

Copyright © 1978 by College Entrance Examination Board. All rights reserved.
Library of Congress Catalog Card Number: 78-59153
Printed in the United States of America

Contents

Preface.	1
Organization of the Bibliography.	3
I. Sources of Program Information	
A. General Information about Aid Programs and Institutions	4
B. Information about Programs for Specific Student Groups.	8
C. Information about Programs in Specific States.	10
II. The History, Philosophy, and Purpose of Aid	
A. History	12
B. Philosophy and Purpose	14
III. Financial Aid Administration, Management, and Problems	
A. General	24
B. Need Analysis Systems and Issues	34
C. Student Expenses and Expense Budgets	46
D. Student Aid Counseling and Information Services	48
E. Packaging Aid Awards.	51
F. Data Processing in Student Aid	53
G. Scholarships, Grants, and Education Benefits.	55
H. Loans	59
I. Employment and Work-Study Programs	67
J. Programs for Special Student Groups	70
K. Aid Administration at Specific Types of Institutions	77
L. Financial Aid Program Annual Reports	80
IV. Financial Aid Administration as a Profession	
A. Characteristics of Aid Administrators	85
B. Training and Professional Development	88
C. Activities of Professional Associations.	90
V. Federal and State Issues and Problems in Student Aid	92
VI. Financial Aid and Financing Postsecondary Education	105
VII. Research on Financial Aid	
A. Student Access, Choice, Retention, Attrition, and Achievement and Aid Needs	123
B. Scholarships, Grants, and Education Benefits.	132
C. Loans and Loan Programs	137
D. Employment and Work-Study Programs	140
E. Statewide Financial Aid Studies.	143
F. Studies Concerning Special Student Groups	153
G. Tuition and Student Expenses.	163

Preface

One of the critical elements of a profession is that the knowledge and skills of its practitioners flow from and are supported by a body of knowledge that has been organized into an internally consistent system. This collective body of knowledge is characterized as "the literature of the profession." As the practice of financial aid administration in the United States has evolved into the financial aid profession, so too has the literature of financial aid grown. What has been lacking is the systematic organization of that literature into a *source* to which interested students, administrators, educators, policymakers, and others could turn for information.

This document is intended as a sourcebook for anyone interested in learning more about financial aid and related matters.

Many financial aid documents are prepared and published by research bureaus or other agencies as single, isolated events. Relatively few groups publish aid-related items on a continuing basis. Consequently, the literature contains many fugitive documents whose impact is lost because other researchers are unaware of their existence. One purpose of this collection is to bring as much of this fugitive literature as possible into one location so that its content will not continue to be lost to others. Although considerable effort has been expended to make this collection complete, some items have inevitably escaped detection. The compilers apologize for oversights and urge those who identify gaps to communicate the appropriate references for inclusion in subsequent volumes.

To be included in this collection an item had to be accessible through collegiate libraries, the facilities of the ERIC (Educational Resources Information Center) Clearinghouse on Higher Education, federal libraries, or publishers. The items were identified through references such as the *Education Index*, the listings of the Congressional Information Services, the *Monthly Catalogue of U.S. Government Publications, Dissertation Abstracts International*, the *Bulletin of Public Affairs Information Service*, and the ERIC Clearinghouse services. In most instances, items were reviewed for the abstracts. In a few cases, when material was not readily available, secondary sources were used to prepare the annotations.

Most of the documents cited were published after 1969. Earlier materials were included if they had not been made obsolete by changes in the aid profession or the programs it administers. Some early items of continuing historical interest have been retained. It should be noted that the literature published prior to 1970 is sparse. Before that time, aid appears to have been of less critical interest to educational researchers and writers.

We gratefully acknowledge the support and interest of James E. Nelson, vice president for research and development at the College Board, and Robert J. Kates, Jr., vice president for student assistance services, whose interest made this document possible.

Jerry S. Davis
William D. Van Dusen

Brookdale, California
September 1977

Organization of the Bibliography

The references and annotations in this bibliography are organized into seven major categories based on their primary contents or emphasis:

I. Sources of Program Information
II. The History, Philosophy, and Purpose of Aid
III. Financial Aid Administration, Management, and Problems
IV. Financial Aid Administration as a Profession
V. Federal and State Issues and Problems in Student Aid
VI. Financial Aid and Financing Postsecondary Education
VII. Research on Financial Aid

Assignment to a category was, in some instances, arbitrary. When an item dealt with several topics, it was placed in the category that appeared to represent its dominant theme. If doubts persisted, practicing aid administrators were consulted and their judgment governed.

Almost all categories and subcategories are preceded by descriptions of the major themes and contents of its items. These descriptions should make it easier for readers to find specific items related to their interests.

I. Sources of Program Information

The first question that can be asked about financial aid is "what is it?" At the most basic level, financial aid is the total of the aid programs available to students enrolled in postsecondary institutions in the United States. The proliferation of student aid programs has been described as "one of the delightful wonders and one of the frightening horrors of . . . higher education in the United States." It is a delight because it provides resources in support of the diversity of students, courses of study, interests, and institutions characteristic of our postsecondary educational system; it is a horror because it severely complicates the task of counseling students about all the available aid resources to which they might apply.

This chapter lists guidebooks that describe the variety of aid resources.

I.A. General Information about Aid Programs and Institutions

The entries in this section consist of general guides to institutional, state, federal and private aid programs available to the majority of present and potential students. Most of the guides include descriptions of award criteria, application procedures and deadlines, and addresses from which additional information or applications can be secured. Each guide is organized in a different way, but all provide persons interested in receiving financial aid with the information needed to make application for it. The entries will be of interest to those responsible for counseling prospective and current students, to students seeking information on aid sources, and to those who are interested in an overview of available financial aid resources.

I.A.1. American Legion. *Need a lift?* Indianapolis, Ind.: American Legion, 1972.
  Provides career and financial aid information for all students. Organized by state.

I.A.2. Brownstein, S. C. and Weiner, M. *You can win a scholarship.* Woodbury, N. Y.: Barron's Educational Series Inc., 1972.
  Lists general and specific scholarships made available by colleges, by state and federal governments, and by private organizations.

I.A.3. Burke, Y. B. Financial aids for postsecondary education: An update. *Journal of Student Financial Aid,* Vol. 5, March 1975, pp. 32–49.
  Describes available financial aid and application procedures.

I.A.4. Cass, J. and Birnbaum, M. *Comparative guide to American Colleges.* New York: Harper & Row, Publishers, 1973.

Provides narrative descriptions of all accredited four-year colleges, including information on admissions requirements, academic environments, campus life, costs and available aid.

I.A.5. Chronicle Guidance Publications, Inc. *Scholarships, loans, and awards offered by the 50 states, District of Columbia, and Puerto Rico.* Student Aid Bulletin, Vol. 27, No. 1, 1975–76. Moravia, N.Y.: Chronicle Guidance Publications, Inc., 1975.

Lists current sources of aid available to students in each state.

I.A.6. Chronicle Guidance Publications, Inc. *Student Aid Annual, 1975–1976.* Moravia, N.Y.: Chronicle Guidance Publications, Inc., 1975.

Contains information on aid programs offered nationally or regionally by noncollegiate public and private sources. Covers freshman through postdoctoral programs.

I.A.7. College Entrance Examination Board. *Admissions, financial aid, and placement procedures at colleges that use College Board services, 1976.* New York: College Entrance Examination Board, 1976.

Describes the policies and procedures of over 1,500 colleges that use College Board services. Organized by state.

I.A.8. College Scholarship Service. *Meeting college costs in 1977–78: A guide for students and parents.* New York: College Entrance Examination Board, 1976. (Revised annually)

Helps students and parents to determine if the student is qualified for aid, to estimate educational costs, and to estimate what parents may be asked to pay toward college expenses.

I.A.9. Congressional Research Service. *Federal and state student aid programs, 1972.* Washington, D.C.: Government Printing Office, 1972.

Describes federal and state programs by types for graduate and undergraduate students for various courses of study. Lists publications and sources of additional information.

I.A.10. Cox, C. *How to beat the high cost of college.* New York: Bernard Geis Associates, Random House, Inc., 1971.

Provides students with information on where and how to get financial aid from public and private sources.

I.A.11. Feingold, S. N. *Scholarships, fellowships, and loans, Vol. 5.* Arlington, Mass.: Bellman Publishing Company, 1972.

Describes available aid by vocational goals and by state and geographic locations. Notes requirements of sex, racial-ethnic groups, membership in labor unions, etc.

I.A.12. Gillete, P. J. (Ed.) *Complete guide to student financial aid.* Hauppauge, N.Y.: Universal Publishing and Distributing Corp., 1971.

Lists names and addresses of federal, state, and private aid programs. Divided into three sections—aid for undergraduates, aid for graduate students, and advice to high school students who are considering college.

I.A.13. Keeslar, O. *Financial aids for higher education, 1976-1977 Catalogue.* Dubuque, Iowa: William C. Brown Co., 1976.

Lists all types of college aid available. Written for counselors and students.

I.A.14. Lever. W. E. *How to obtain money for college.* New York: Arco Publishing Co., Inc., 1976.

Contains advice on determining college costs and estimating parental contributions; lists aid sources by program, state, and institution.

I.A.15. Life Insurance Agency Management Association. *1976-77 college costs.* Hartford, Conn.: LIAMA, 1976. (Published annually)

Contains data on student costs at over 2,000 institutions.

I.A.16. Mathies, M. L. (Ed.) *The college blue book—Scholarships, fellowships, grants, and loans.* New York: Macmillan, Inc., 1975.

Lists award programs by subject area: general, humanities, social services, sciences, health and medical sciences, area studies, and specialized programs. Gives the number, type, and amounts of awards offered by each program; includes application deadlines and where to write for further information.

I.A.17. *National register of scholarships and fellowships.* New York: Monarch Press, 1975.

Describes programs and funds by source (national private organizations, federal agencies) and geographically by state. Includes a general alphabetical index.

I.A.18. Proia, N. C. and DiGaspari, V. M. *Barron's handbook of American college financial aid.* Woodbury, N.Y.: Barron's Educational Series Inc., 1974.

Contains data charts on available grants and loans and how to apply for them.

I.A.19. Proia, N. C. *Barron's handbook of college transfer information.* Woodbury, N.Y.: Barron's Educational Series Inc., 1975.

A guide to the transfer process including state-by-state charts with information on admissions, transfer of credits, and financial assistance.

I.A.20. Proia, N. C. and DiGaspari, V. M. *Barron's handbook of junior and community college financial aid.* Woodbury, N.Y.: Barron's Educational Series Inc., 1974.

Contains data charts on financial aid offered at more than 900 two-year colleges. Describes grants and loans available and how to apply for them.

I.A.21. Searles, A., Jr. and Scott, A. *Guide to financial aids for students in arts and sciences, for graduate and professional study.* New York: Arco Publishing Co., Inc., 1974.

Lists programs and funds for graduate and professional education by general and specific areas of study.

I.A.22. Suchar, E. W. and Harris, P. *The official College Entrance Examination Board financial aid guide for students and parents.* New York: Simon & Schuster, Inc., 1975.

Describes types of aid available and how to apply for them. Contains checklists, sample letters, and timetables for applications. Chapters describe sources of aid: parents and family, institutions, states, the federal Basic Educational Opportunity Grants (BEOG) Program, the federal Guaranteed Student Loan Program (GSLP), special sources such as benefits, and aid from local programs.

I.A.23. UNESCO. *Study abroad.* New York: Unipub, 1974.

A compilation of international scholarships and courses sponsored or administered by international and national organizations and institutions.

I.A.24. U.S. Congress, Senate Committee on Labor and Public Welfare. *Federal and state student aid programs, 1972* (Including the Education Amendments of 1972). Washington, D.C.: Government Printing office, 1972.

A state-by-state description of federal and state aid programs for postsecondary education.

I.A.25. U.S. Office of Education. *Major federal student assistance programs administered by the Office of Education.* Washington, D.C.: Department of Health, Education, and Welfare, 1974.

Summarizes types and amounts of assistance, eligibility requirements, and application procedures for federal student assistance programs administered by the Office of Education.

I.A.26. U.S. Office of Education. *We can work it out: Talent Search, Upward Bound, Special Services.* Washington, D.C.: Department of Health, Education, and Welfare, 1975.

A guide to assistance and services offered by the Office of Education's "trio" programs.

I.A.27. Watts, S. F. (Ed.) *The college handbook.* New York: College Entrance Examination Board, 1977.

Detailed descriptions of 2,049 colleges include information on size, location, calendar, curriculum, admissions requirements, student life, costs, and financial aid. Also provides brief data on 829 other colleges.

I.B. Information about Programs for Specific Student Groups

Some student aid programs administer restricted funds that are limited to students with particular characteristics. The entries in this section describe aid available to special groups such as foreign students, racial and ethnic minorities, and those interested in particular careers or fields of study. Like the general guides, these references typically provide application criteria, procedures, and addresses to which students can address inquiries.

I. B. 1. American Library Association. *Financial assistance for library education, 1976–1977.* Chicago: American Library Association, 1975.

Lists financial aid awards greater than $500 from state library agencies, national and state library associations, local libraries, and postsecondary institutions for undergraduate and graduate study in library education.

I. B. 2. Chronicle Guidance Publications, Inc. *Scholarships, loans, and awards offered by independent and AFL-CIO affiliated labor unions.* Student Aid Bulletin, Vol. 27, No. 2, 1975–76. Moravia, N.Y.: Chronicle Guidance Publications, Inc., 1975.

Lists union-sponsored scholarships and loans from programs of national and international unions awarded on a national basis and those of council, district, and local unions.

I. B. 3. College Entrance Examination Board. *Entering higher education in the United States: A guide for students from other countries.* New York: College Entrance Examination Board, 1974.

Discusses problems foreign students encounter in seeking information and making decisions about attending a college in the United States. Offers several sources of information for students.

I. B. 4. College Entrance Examination Board. *Financial planning for study in the United States.* New York: College Entrance Examination Board, 1976.

Written for foreign students who plan to study in the United States. Includes data on application and testing fees, travel, tuition, housing, expenses for married students and dependents, medical services, kinds of aid available to foreign students, awards from the United States government, and awards from private associations.

I. B. 5. Council for Exceptional Children. *Professional training programs for personnel in special education.* Reston, Va.: Information Center on Exceptional Children, 1974.

Provides information on aid for careers in special education. Includes a listing of 18 sources of career information, information on paraprofessional training, a listing of state directors of special education, and a listing of over 350 teacher-training programs.

I. B. 6. Drummond, C. E. *Going right on: Information and advice for minority students who want to continue their education after high school.* New York: College Entrance Examination Board, 1976.
Guide to postsecondary education for minority students. Describes admissions and financial aid application procedures, methods of choosing colleges, and sources of additional information.

I. B. 7. Educational Testing Service. *Graduate and professional school opportunities for minority students.* Princeton, N.J.: Educational Testing Service, 1971.
A guide to educational and financial opportunities for minority students at 740 postsecondary institutions.

I. B. 8. Health Resources Administration. *How to pay for your health career education: a guide for minority students.* Bethesda, Md.: Public Health Service, 1974.
Discusses the need for more minority workers in health occupations. Lists public and private sources that help minority students plan and pay for their education in health fields.

I. B. 9. Kingsbury, W. T. and Mckinley, F. *Financing college education for Indians.* Tempe, Ariz.: National Indian Training and Research Center, 1971.
Lists financial aid programs that provide assistance to Native Americans in postsecondary education.

I. B. 10. National funds, fellowships, and foundations in journalism. *Journalism Educator,* Vol. 30, January 1976, pp. 91–92.
Lists sources of financial aid for study in the journalism-mass communications area.

I. B. 11. Noon, J. *The Navajo way: from high school to college.* Window Rock, Ariz.: DNA Legal Services, Inc., 1975.
A guide to entering college. Discusses choosing a college, admissions procedures, financial aid sources and applications, miscellaneous forms which must be completed, and a timetable for applying to college.

I. B. 12. Peterson, P. Assistantships and fellowships in agricultural education, 1976–77. *Agricultural Education Magazine,* Vol. 48, March 1976, pp. 209–210.
Information on aid to graduate students in agricultural education. Includes data on types of assistantships, number available, work expected, remuneration, source of funds, deadlines, and persons to contact.

I. B. 13. Stratton, B., et al. *College level financial aid opportunities for migrant students within the State University of New York.* Albany, N.Y.: New York State Education Department, Bureau of Migrant Education, 1975.
Assists guidance counselors and administrators in identifying financial aid programs that aid migrant students in entering college within the SUNY system.

I. B. 14. The Newspaper Fund. *1974 journalism scholarship guide.* Princeton, N.J.: The Newspaper Fund, Inc., 1973.

Lists aid available for students enrolled in journalism or communications programs. Lists aid offered through colleges and by newspapers and professional societies.

I.B. 15. U.S. Bureau of Indian Affairs. *Career development opportunities for Native Americans.* Washington, D.C.: Department of the Interior, 1975.

Contains information about aid to Native Americans seeking a college education. Describes various adult educational and vocational-technical opportunities.

I.B. 16. Wilson, M. S. *Financial aid for minorities in business.* Garrett Park, Md.: Garrett Park Press, 1975.

A guide to institutional, private, and governmental aid for minority students interested in business vocations and programs.

I.B. 17. Wilson, M. S. *Financial aid for minorities in education.* Garrett Park, Md.: Garrett Park Press, 1975.

A guide to institutional, private, and governmental aid for minority students interested in becoming teachers.

I.B. 18. Wilson, M. S. *Financial aid for minorities in journalism and communication.* Garrett Park, Md.: Garrett Park Press, 1975.

A guide to institutional, private, and governmental aid for minority students interested in careers in journalism and mass communications.

I.B. 19. Wilson, M. S. *Financial aid for minorities in law.* Garrett Park, Md.: Garrett Park Press, 1975.

A guide to financial assistance for minority students interested in law careers.

I.C. Information about Programs in Specific States

In recent years, a number of public and private agencies in the various states have collected data about financial aid programs and procedures for residents of their state. In some cases, these guides are limited to state programs; others provide information on general aid programs. The entries in this section will be of interest both to student residents of the states covered and to agencies in other states interested in producing comparable documents. Generally the guides are published by planning, governing, or coordinating agencies.

I.C. 1. Iowa State Higher Education Facilities Commission. *Student guide to financial aid.* Des Moines, Iowa: Iowa State Higher Education Facilities Commission, 1977.

Describes financial aid available to attend public and private postsecondary institutions in the state.

I.C.2. Maryland Council for Higher Education. *Admissions and financial aid information for Maryland's public and private postsecondary educational institutions.* Annapolis, Md.: Maryland Council for Higher Education, 1975.

Describes admissions requirements, tuitions and required fees, program offerings and financial aid available to Maryland residents at public and private colleges in the state.

I.C.3. New York State Education Department. *Handbook on scholarships and grants.* Albany: New York State Education Department, 1974.

Designed for high school and college personnel responsible for advising students on grant and scholarship programs administered by the New York State Education Department.

I.C.4. North Dakota Higher Education Facilities Commission. *A Guide to postsecondary educational opportunities in North Dakota.* Bismarck, N. Dak.: North Dakota Higher Education Facilities Commission, 1976.

Describes institutional admissions and financial aid application procedures, types of aid by sources, and postsecondary aid programs available in the state.

I.C.5. North Dakota Student Financial Assistance Agency. *Student financial aid handbook.* Bismarck, N. Dak.: North Dakota Student Financial Assistance Agency, 1976.

Information on federal, state, and institutional aid for students attending postsecondary institutions in the state.

I.C.6. Ohio College Association. *Toward college in Ohio, 1977-78.* Columbus: Ohio College Association, 1976.

Contains admissions and financial aid information on postsecondary institutions in Ohio.

I.C.7. University of Wyoming, Higher Education Council, Community College Commission. *Student financial aid at Wyoming colleges.* Cheyenne, Wyo.: Wyoming Higher Education Council, 1976.

Information for students on aid available to attend postsecondary institutions in the state.

I.C.8. West Virginia Board of Regents. *Financial aid resources available to students attending West Virginia colleges and universities.* Charleston, W. Va.: West Virginia Board of Regents, 1974.

Student guide to financial aid resources at postsecondary institutions in the state.

II. The History, Philosophy, and Purpose of Aid

Although the literature of financial aid is a relatively recent development there have been aid programs since early colonial days. The first recorded aid program was established at Harvard College in 1643. The federal government entered the student aid field during the depression when the National Youth Administration sponsored student employment programs. The profession of aid administration, however, did not thrive until 1958 with the passage of the National Defense Act. For the first time every college and university in the United States had access to substantial amounts of federal money in support of student aid. Institutions, which in the past had treated aid as a minor adjunct to academic or business offices, appointed individuals specifically responsible for aid administration. As these practitioners undertook their duties, they began to develop and document their activities.

This chapter identifies documents dealing with the development of the financial aid profession — its history, the philosophical foundations on which it is based, and what it seeks to accomplish.

II.A. History

For as long as there have been colleges in the United States, there has been financial aid to help students attend them. Prior to World War II, student aid was primarily distributed by the institutions themselves, either from their own or from private resources. The period after 1945 saw a massive infusion of federal and state funds. Today, the federal budget for student aid exceeds $2.9 billion. The items in this section describe the history of those developments.

Three references discuss the general history and development of student aid programs (Beck, 1971; Godzicki, 1975; Nash, 1968). One article deals with the early history of aid (Allmendinger, 1971). Three discuss the development of state aid programs (Boyd, 1975; Giddens, 1970; Meade, 1972); four concentrate on federal programs (Green, 1971; Kaufman, 1972; McCormick, 1972; Sanders, 1975); and one examines institutional aid (Moon, 1975). One of the more interesting items is a dissertation on the history of financial aid at a single institution (Gray, 1976).

II.A.1. Allmendinger, D. F. The strangeness of the American Education Society: Indigent students and the new charity, 1815–1840. *History of Education Quarterly*, Vol. 11, Spring 1971, pp. 3–22.

States that one of the major purposes of aid to indigent students in the early 1800s was to help staff the pulpits of New England churches.

II.A.2. Beck, N. E. *A history of modern student financial aids*. Muncie, Ind.: Ball State University, 1971. (Dissertation)

Discusses the growth of student aid programs within the contexts of changes in financial support of higher education (from appropriations to institutions to support of students) and concern for efficiency and equity.

II.A.3. Boyd, J. D. History of state involvement in financial aid. In *Perspectives on financial aid*, New York: College Entrance Examination Board, 1975.

Brief description of the history, characteristics, and goals of state-supported student aid programs. Discusses different types of state programs and their purposes.

II.A.4. Giddens, T. R. Origins of state scholarship programs: 1647–1913. *College and University*, Vol. 46, Fall 1970, pp. 37–45.

Describes the early history and development of state-supported financial aid programs.

II.A.5. Godzicki, R. J. A history of financial aids in the United States. In *Money, marbles, or chalk: Student financial support in higher education*. Keene, R., Adams, F. C., and King, J. E. (Eds.) Carbondale, Ill.: Southern Illinois University Press, 1975.

Provides a brief history of the development of financial aid programs and their underlying concepts.

II.A.6. Gray, C. E. *Student financial support at Southern Illinois University at Carbondale: 1874–1974*. Carbondale, Ill.: Southern Illinois University, 1976. (Dissertation)

A study of student financial support programs at one university and the internal and external factors contributing to their growth and development.

II.A.7. Green, E. Federal student aid: Past, present, and future. *Journal of Student Financial Aid*, Vol. 1, May 1971, pp. 14–21.

Provides brief analysis of changes in college costs and enrollments and the federal response in terms of student aid. Describes the aid approaches favored by the author.

II.A.8. Kaufman, M. L. Federal aid to education, 1867–1971. *Journal of Education*, Vol. 154, February 1972, pp. 25–31.

A discussion of the history and underlying rationale of federal support to education.

II.A.9. McCormick, J. L. The role of the federal government in student financial aid — A history. *Journal of Student Financial Aid*, Vol. 2, March 1972, pp. 47–56.

Brief history of financial aid from 1879 to the present. Focuses attention on growth of federal programs and federal involvement since World War II.

II.A.10. Meade, R. C. The development and significance of state scholarship programs. *Journal of student Financial Aid,* Vol. 2, March 1972, pp. 41–46.

Traces the development and impact of state student grant programs from the Civil War to the present.

II.A.11. Moon, R. G., Jr. History of institutional financial aid in the United States. In *Perspectives on financial aid.* New York: College Entrance Examination Board, 1975.

Brief discussion of the history of college financial aid programs. Categorizes institutional aid problems: selection, management, accountability, and professionalization of aid administrators.

II.A.12. Nash, G. The history and growth of student financial aid. *Journal of the National Association of College Admissions Counselors,* Vol. 13, November 1968, pp. 11–16.

Provides a brief history of student financial aid, focusing on developments since World War II.

II.A.13. Sanders, E. History of federal involvement in financial aid. In *Perspectives on Financial Aid.* New York: College Entrance Examination Board, 1975.

Brief discussion of legislation and programs that have increased federal role in student aid. The author argues that there is no single, clear-cut rationale for federal aid to students.

II.B. Philosophy and Purpose

There is widespread consensus that the purpose of financial aid is to help students who could not otherwise afford to attend postsecondary institutions. The three generally accepted goals of aid programs are to enhance student access to, choice of, and retention in postsecondary education. However, when it comes to making choices about who should receive what kinds of aid from which sources to attend what kinds of institutions, the degree of consensus among policymakers declines. The literature in this section addresses these issues.

Two early documents are collections of papers on the role of financial aid in achieving national and institutional goals (College Entrance Examination Board, 1962, 1963). These provide excellent background data on the relationships between financial aid programs, program effects, and educational policy.

Several items are concerned with the role of financial aid in enhancing equal opportunity or equal access to postsecondary education for children from less-affluent families. There are four collections of papers on the financial aid needs of poor minority students (College Entrance Examination Board, 1970, 1971, 1973; Fleming, 1975). A fifth collection discusses educational opportunity for all students at all levels (U.S. Congress, 1971). Cartter (1971b) discusses the costs and benefits of universal higher education. Two items are concerned with access in specific geographic areas — Canada (Peitchinis, 1973) and the state of Mississippi (Woodward, 1975).

Saurman (1972) and Katz (1971) maintain that the nation is not doing enough to enhance educational opportunity for all students. Hansen (1970) discusses the effect of family income, educational costs, and available aid on college attendance. Three studies indicate that aid opportunities are better for some students than for others. (Schlekat, 1968; Seymour, et al., 1972; Sidar, 1974). Others believe that financial need is only *one* of the significant barriers to equal access and that these barriers limit the impact of financial aid. Ferrin (1970) describes the financial barrier but indicates that attitudinal, academic, and geographic barriers may be equally significant. Fuller (1976) suggests that the nonfinancial barriers are *more* significant than the financial ones.

Gross (1966) suggests that one reason the impact of aid programs is limited is because their real purpose is to enhance institutional survival, not to assist financially handicapped students. Others suggest that the effects of financial aid are limited by a lack of consistent and coordinated policies and programs (Fife, 1975; Owen, 1970); by a lack of adequate program funding (Bloss, et al., 1970); and by a lack of institutional support (Walkup and Hoyt, 1975). The Panel on Student Financial Need Analysis (Cartter, 1971a) offers a number of reasons why the impact of aid is limited and suggests ways in which new methods of need analysis and the packaging of student aid awards might help to alleviate these conditions. Ostar (1976) believes that the best way to enhance equal opportunity is by maintaining low tuitions, not by increasing financial aid.

Two articles describe radical approaches to solving financial aid problems and enhancing equal opportunity. Hatch (1969) proposes a National Need and Merit Award program which would provide students with monetary entitlements based on a combination of merit and need — the greater the merit and need, the higher the entitlement. Tobin and Ross (1969) propose a National Youth Endowment Program under which students could borrow for any educational or training purpose and repay their loans through federal taxes over a lifetime of earning.

Concern about who should receive aid is expressed in nearly all the literature in this section. This topic generates the most controversy in relation to "emancipated" students, students who are no longer dependent on their parents for financial support. Providing aid to these students is controversial because it is almost universally believed that parents have a responsibility to pay for as much of their children's educational costs as they can reasonably afford. There is disagreement on who should be considered independent, how the financial needs of independent students should be measured, what types and amounts of aid should be awarded to them, and how these policy issues relate to equity in the administration of aid and the financing of postsecondary education.

Five references in this section deal with awarding aid to independent students. Seward (1972) believes that equity in financial aid cannot be achieved as long as parents of some students are relieved of their responsibility to meet some educational costs. Curtis (1974), Sidar (1973), and Windham (1974) examine the various criteria for determining independent status and their implications for the financial support of students and institutions. Hensley (1974) reports on a study of policies regarding independent student status and aid practices at many western universities.

Additional items discuss support of graduate students (Kidd, 1970, 1974; Miller, 1973); support of students who disrupt campus activities (Harrison, et al., 1971); support of part-time students (Sims and Andrews, 1976); and the awarding of aid to students who demonstrate no financial aid needs (Sidar, 1976; Wilcox, 1973-74).

II.B.1. Bloss, A. M., et al. Effectiveness of financial aid in equalizing educational opportunities. *College and University,* Vol. 45, Summer 1970, pp. 780-786.

Reports a panel discussion on this topic. The panel agreed that equal opportunity had not yet been achieved by aid programs, primarily due to lack of sufficient funding.

II.B.2. Cartter, A. M. (Chairman) *New approaches to student financial aid: Report of the Panel on Student Financial Need Analysis.* New York: College Entrance Examination Board, 1971a.

Report of the panel's evaluations and recommendations on college admissions and financial aid policies, financial aid attitudes of users, adequacy of College Scholarship Service (css) need analysis procedures for minority/poverty students, technical changes to improve equity in need assessment, and the packaging of student aid awards.

II.B.3. Cartter, A. M. Student financial aid. *Universal higher education: Costs and benefits.* Washington, D.C.: American Council of Education, 1971b.

Distinguishes between three types of equal opportunity or access: equal opportunity with merit constraints, universal access to some form of postsecondary education, and universal college education. Discusses the financial aid costs of achieving each goal and describes a financial system in which education costs would be divided into fourths: one-fourth paid by the federal government, one-fourth paid by states and private gifts and endowments, one-fourth paid by parents, and one-fourth by students from self-help and long-term loans.

II.B.4. College Entrance Examination Board. *Barriers to higher education.* New York: College Entrance Examination Board, 1971.

Collection of articles on obstacles to access to higher education faced by minority/poverty students. Discusses organization of higher education, abuses of testing, lack of financial resources, and special programs for minority youth.

II.B.5. College Entrance Examination Board. *Financing equal opportunity in higher education.* New York: College Entrance Examination Board, 1970.

Report on a 1969 colloquium examines barriers to higher education for minority/poverty students. Possible solutions to the problems are offered.

II.B.6. College Entrance Examination Board. *Student financial aid and institutional purpose.* New York: College Entrance Examination Board, 1963.

Collection of papers on the relationships between financial aid policies and practices and institutional goals and purposes.

II.B.7. College Entrance Examination Board. *Student financial aid and national purpose.* New York: College Entrance Examination Board, 1962.

Collection of papers on the role of student financial aid in achieving national goals for postsecondary education.

II.B.8. College Entrance Examination Board. *Toward equal opportunity for higher education: Report of the panel on financing low-income and minority students in higher education.* New York: College Entrance Examination Board, 1973.

Report of a panel's findings and recommendations regarding financial problems of minority/poverty student access to higher education.

II.B.9. Curtis, G. *Who should support the non-traditional aid applicant?* Speech, 1974. (ERIC: ED 090817; HE 005395)

Discusses issues involved in the determination of self-supporting student status. Argues that parental income data should be requested for students up to age 25.

II.B.10. Ferrin, R. I. *Barriers to universal higher education.* Palo Alto, Calif.: Access Research Office, College Entrance Examination Board, 1970.

Presents research findings on four major barriers to access to postsecondary education: attitudinal, academic, geographic, and financial barriers.

II.B.11. Fife, J. D. *Applying the goals of student financial aid.* Washington, D.C.: American Association for Higher Education, 1975.

States that the distribution of funds to financial aid programs causes them to fall short of achievement of their purposes. To achieve a more equitable system: (1) students must be assured that financial aid will be available; (2) announcement of aid and awards should be made before students have to choose colleges; (3) the determination of student need must be based on one need-analysis method; and (4) sufficient funds should be provided to meet the needs thus determined.

II.B.12. Fleming, V. (Ed.) *Financial barriers to equal access in higher education.* Atlanta: Southern Education Foundation, 1975.

The issue of financing postsecondary education is discussed from the viewpoint of providing minority/poverty students with access to postsecondary education in southern states.

II.B.13. Fritz, A., et al. Future of financial aid. *College and University,* Vol. 51, Summer 1976, pp. 755–757.

Report on a panel discussion on the topic. Trends mentioned include challenges to legality of aid, increased governmental intervention, and the rise of consumerism.

II.B.14. Fuller, B. Increasing student financial aid programs: A misdirected means of expanding access? *Research in Higher Education,* Vol. 5, No. 1, 1976, pp. 27–38.

Data on students in the Los Angeles area indicate that providing additional financial aid may have a diminishing effect on access to postsecondary education. Suggests that other barriers may be more significant.

II.B.15. Green, E. The disadvantaged middle class. *National Association of College Admissions Counselors Journal,* Vol. 18, November 1973, pp. 1–4.

Discusses recent trends in need analysis and the distribution of financial aid that discriminate against students from middle-income families.

II.B.16. Gross, S. J. A critique of practices in the administration of financial aid. *Journal of College Student Personnel,* March 1966, pp. 78–85.

Examines the administration of student aid from the student personnel workers' viewpoint. Believes that the purpose of financial aid, in practice, is to help institutions survive, not to assist financially handicapped students.

II.B.17. Halfmoon, R. T. Position paper on financial aid. *American Indian Culture Center,* Vol. 3, Fall/Winter 1971–72, pp. 26–27.

Discusses the Native American student's need for financial aid and aid services.

II.B.18. Hansen, W. L. An examination of financial barriers to college attendance. In *Trends in postsecondary education.* Washington, D.C.: U.S. Office of Education, 1970.

Examines the impact of family income and related factors on college attendance, college costs, and the availability of financial aid.

II.B.19. Harrison, R. J., et al. Financial aids for the disrupter. *College and University,* Vol. 46, Summer 1971, pp. 617–620.

Report on a panel discussion on the topic. It was agreed that denying aid to disruptive students who were still eligible to be enrolled was a discriminatory practice.

II. B. 20. Hatch, W. T. Could this financial aid plan help end student unrest? *College Board Review,* No. 72, Summer 1969, pp. 18–25.

Proposes a national Need and Merit Award program which would provide high school graduates with monetary entitlements (based on income and class rank) to be used for expenditure in any educational or training program of their choice. Believes such a program would enhance freedom of choice, encourage high achievement, and reduce student alienation.

II. B. 21. Henry, J. B. Trends in student financial aid. *Journal of College Student Personnel,* Vol. 10, July 1969, pp. 226–231.

Reviews trends in the philosophy and structure of student aid. Discusses trends in equal educational opportunity, shifts in the distribution of aid to different students, and the growth of state aid programs.

II. B. 22. Hensley, M. R. The self-supporting student: Trends and implications. *Journal of Student Financial Aid,* Vol. 4, June 1974, pp. 23–29.

Report on a study of self-supporting students at colleges in the western region. Concerned with increasing enrollment of these students, their financial resources, and the consequent administrative problems in the distribution of financial aid.

II. B. 23. Hunter, R. D. Tuition equalization grant program. *Compact,* Vol. 5, December 1971, pp. 31–32.

Describes a new program in Texas to provide financial aid to private college students, and discusses the questions behind its development.

II. B. 24. Katz, B. D. Equal opportunity – do we really mean it? *Compact,* Vol. 5, October 1971, pp. 6–7.

Argues that our postsecondary educational system has been created to educate middle-class America, with services to low-income students being disproportionately low.

II. B. 25. Kidd, C. V. Federal support for graduate education reexamined. *Educational Record,* Vol. 51, Fall 1970, pp. 339–346.

Assesses the strengths and weaknesses of the present system of federal support to graduate education and discusses some alternatives to that system. The need for a stronger structural support of research and graduate education in the executive branch is discussed.

II. B. 26. Kidd, C. V. Graduate education: The new debate. *Change,* Vol. 6, May 1974, pp. 43–50.

Critical review of several reports (published since 1969) on support of graduate education.

II. B. 27. Marmaduke, A. S. Who will pay for college? *Journal of Student Financial Aid,* Vol. 1, May 1971, pp. 22–27.

Discusses the economic reasons why students, their parents, and society should share the costs of higher education. The author believes that future students will be asked to bear the greatest burden and suggests that the potential impact of this trend on students should be studied.

II.B.28. Miller, J. Portable grants for graduate study. *Change,* Vol. 4, October 1973, pp. 50–51.

Report on a task force sponsored by the Department of Health, Education, and Welfare. Recommends that federal funds for graduate study be given directly to students in the form of portable fellowships.

II.B.29. O'Hearne, J. J. Financial aid may help most by helping fewer students. *College and University Business,* Vol. 49, August 1970, pp. 37–39.

An analysis of how student aid can best be distributed and packaged to suit the needs of both students and institutions.

II.B.30. Ostar, A. W. Why I'm for low tuition. AGB *Report,* Vol. 18, July/August 1976, pp. 18–20.

Maintains that student aid is less effective than low tuitions in increasing access to higher education.

II.B.31. Owen, J. D. *Toward a more consistent, socially relevant college scholarships policy.* Baltimore, Md.: Center for the Study of Social Organization of Schools, The Johns Hopkins University, 1970.

This study argues that the existing system of aid to students is chaotic and inconsistent. Proposes a plan using cost-benefit analysis to attain national objectives.

II.B.32. Peitchinis, S. G. Equality and inequality of opportunity: The financing of postsecondary education in Canada. *Australian Journal of Higher Education,* Vol. 5, December 1973, pp. 64–75.

Proposes the establishement of an integrated student aid system consisting of a combination of unconditional grants, loans, conditional grants, and scholarships to increase educational opportunity in Canada.

II.B.33. Pesqueira, R. E. Equal opportunity in higher education: Choice as well as access. *College Board Review,* No. 97, Fall 1975, pp. 10–13.

Criticizes public policy grounded on the narrow concepts of providing equal financial access to minority/poverty students. Contends that access without the ability to choose among institutions is relatively meaningless.

II.B.34. Prentice, J. T., et al. Financial aid: Direction of the '70's. *College and University,* Vol. 46, Summer 1971, pp. 569–582.

Report on a panel discussion on the potential effects of federal and state financial aid programs on students and institutions. Focuses on governmental goals and objectives.

II.B.35. Saunders, C. B., Jr. The student aid merry-go-round. *Change,* Vol. 8, August 1976, pp. 44–45.

Discusses the conflict between those who favor direct aid to students and those who wish to continue providing aid through postsecondary institutions.

II. B. 36. Saurman, F. S. Minority students: Are we giving them adequate support? *Journal of Student Financial Aid,* Vol. 2, November 1972, pp. 23–31.

Presents some methods and alternatives used by colleges to assist minority students financially, socially, and academically. Describes in detail the programs at Purdue University.

II. B. 37. Schlekat, G. A. Do financial aid programs have a social conscience? *College Board Review,* No. 69, Fall 1968, pp. 15–20.

Analyzes over 10,000 questionnaires from 1,000 colleges surveyed in 1965 to determine what kinds of students received aid of different types and amounts. Analysis found that, although lower-income applicants were more than twice as likely to receive financial aid and in larger amounts than upper-income students, this aid more often included loans and jobs; upper-income students, on the other hand, were more likely to receive grants. The study concludes that lower-income students were more likely to mortgage future eranings and devote more time to employment.

II. B. 38. Seward, C. W., III. An examination of the independent student, the dependent student, and the philosophy of student financial aid. *Journal of Student Financial Aid,* Vol. 2, November 1972, pp. 5–9.

States the impossibility of achieving equity in student financial aid programs from administrative, procedural, or functional standpoints as long as the concept of a financially independent student is considered valid.

II. B. 39. Seymour, W. R., Zimmerman, S. A., and Donato, D. J. Financial aid: What influences who gets it? *Journal of Student Financial Aid,* Vol. 2, November 1972, pp. 10–17.

Reports on a University of Missouri–Columbia study on the relationship of student class level, academic division, residence, home community, and academic ability and achievement to the receipt of financial aid.

II. B. 40. Sidar, A. G., Jr. *No-need awards: An issue.* New York: College Entrance Examination Board, 1976.

Discusses the issues and implications of awarding no-need scholarships to students. Concludes that the practice is ineffective in enhancing student access and choice.

II. B. 41. Sidar, A. G., Jr. Student financial aid: Is there a born loser? *College Board Review,* No. 91, Spring 1974, pp. 24–25.

Maintains that increased access and rising college costs have made program appropriations insufficient to meet all students' needs. Argues that middle-income students are most likely to be neglected in the distribution of aid.

II. B. 42. Sidar, A. G., Jr. What makes a self-supporting student? *College Board Review,* No. 87, Spring 1973, p. 16.

Considers the various criteria for determining a student's independent status for financial aid purposes and examines the implications of alternative criteria.

II.B.43. Sims, E. and Andrews, H. A. The human impact of an adult financial aid program. *Journal of Student Financial Aid,* Vol. 6, May 1976, pp. 9–12.

Reports that aid to adult part-time students has a positive impact on the recipients, their families, and their work lives.

II.B.44. Suchodolski, B. The future of higher education. *Higher Education,* Vol. 3, August 1974, pp. 331–340.

Believes that higher education should offer students the opportunity to combine work and study, that occupational structures should be modified to enable one to advance through study, and that secondary schools should adopt a stronger scientific and occupational orientation.

II.B.45. Tobin, J. and Ross, L. A national youth endowment. *New Republic,* No. 160, May 1969, pp. 18–21.

Proposes a National Youth Endowment Program whereby every American between the ages of 18 and 28 could borrow specified funds for any educational or training purpose. Students would repay their loan through federal income taxes over a lifetime.

II.B.46. Tunis, W. D., et al. Financing a college education. *College and University,* Vol. 50, Summer 1975, pp. 358–361.

Report of a panel discussion on financing a college education. The report makes several predictions about the future of financial aid.

II.B.47. U.S. Congress, Senate Select Committee on Equal Educational Opportunity. *Equal educational opportunity: Hearings before the Select Committee on Equal Educational Opportunity.* Washington, D.C.: Government Printing Office, 1971.

Documents testimony of public and private officials regarding equal opportunity to education at all levels for all segments of society.

II.B.48. Walkup, J. L. and Hoyt, W. G. The institution as an agency of student support. In *Money, marbles, or chalk: Student financial support in higher education.* Keene, R., Adams, F. C., and King, J. E. (Eds.) Carbondale, Ill.: Southern Illinois University Press, 1975.

Discusses the need for development and expansion of institutionally supported student aid programs.

II.B.49. Wilcox, L. Financial aid and admissions quotas. *College Board Review,* No. 90, Winter 1973–74, pp. 10–12.

Examines the relationships between admissions and financial aid policies and the use of monetary awards to attract academically talented students.

II.B.50. Windham, D. M. Need determination and the self-supporting students. *Financial Aid Report,* Vol. 3, No. 3, June 1974.

Discussion of issues concerning definitions of independent students, how they should qualify for assistance, and the forms such assistance should take.

II.B.51. Woodward, J. L. Student aid and access to postsecondary education. In *Five discussions on postsecondary education,* Jobe, E. R. (Ed.) Jackson, Miss.: Mississippi State Postsecondary Planning Board, 1975.

Discusses the relationship between student aid and student access to postsecondary education in Mississippi.

II.B.52. Wren, S. C. *The college student and higher education policy: What stake and what purpose?* Berkeley, Calif.: Carnegie Foundation for the Advancement of Teaching, 1975.

Reports on all proposals of the Carnegie Commission on Higher Education that are of importance and concern to students. Includes chapters on breaking down barriers to equal educational opportunity, college costs and whether students can pay them, the need for expanding educational options, and student participation in governance.

III. Financial Aid Administration, Management, and Problems

This chapter contains a section for general literature on the administration of financial aid programs and additional sections on more specific administrative areas: need analysis systems and issues; student expenses and expense budgets; student counseling and information services; packaging aid awards; the use of data processing in student aid; the administration of scholarship, grant, education benefits, loan, employment, and work-study programs; providing aid to special groups of students; the administration of aid at specific types of institutions; and annual reports of public and private financial aid programs.

III.A. General

A large segment of the literature of financial aid deals with the problems of aid administration and management and with suggestions for improving these processes. While consensus on how best to improve a given situation may be lacking, there is almost total agreement that substantial improvements are needed in many areas.

The majority of the publications listed here are concerned with the real and ideal activities of campus-based aid offices. These studies generally agree that there is a common core of operational activities performed by aid offices on all campuses. This core includes general administration and office management, counseling students about expenses and aid opportunities, development of new or additional aid resources, research and data management activities, and relations with other campus and off-campus agencies.

The most frequently cited work in this category is *A Design for a Model College Financial Aid Office* (Van Dusen and O'Hearne, 1973), a seminal work first published in 1968. The *Final Report* (1975) of the National Task Force on Student Aid Problems provides a comprehensive statement on administrative, managerial, and coordinative problems in student aid. It also contains a series of over 50 specific recommendations to improve the financial aid system. This document provides an excellent starting point for persons new to financial aid who seek a concise overview of the many issues in the administration of aid programs. An earlier statement of the problems leading to the creation of the task force is offered by Marmaduke (1974). Kelly (1977) presents a critical review of the task force recommendations.

For the reader seeking more comprehensive information, a report on the 1974 congressional hearings on higher education legislation covers almost every issue of concern in student financial aid (U.S. Congress, Senate, 1975).

The location of the campus aid office in the organizational structure of the postsecondary institution is the major topic of five of the following items. (Bekking and Stamataros, 1972; De Jarnett, 1975; Edwards and Ingle, 1975; Lovelace, et al., 1976; North, 1975). All of these articles conclude that the aid office should be located in the student personnel services division and that the aid director should report to top college administrators. The authors argue that because financial aid affects matriculation and enrollment of students, it indirectly affects institutional financial strengths and activities. Therefore, the activities of the aid office should be closely monitored by top administrators no less than one level below the chief executive officer on the campus.

Aldmon (1971) and Haines (1976) also believe that financial aid activities are closely related to institutional survival and development. They suggest that the role of financial aid administrators should include participation in long-range institutional planning. Two writers (Elliott, 1974 and Jewett, 1976) present models that can be used in long-range admissions and financial aid planning. Hersey (1973) presents an instructive case study on the strategies and tactics used in developing and implementing new financial aid policies on a college campus.

Four items in this category provide check lists to help financial aid officers evaluate their administrative functions and activities. Bugenhagen, et al. (1976) and Caliendo and Curtice (1977) list criteria for determining whether aid operations correspond with Higher Education Act, Title IX regulations. Hage (1973) lists 37 specific recommendations for improving the management of aid programs. Keene (1975) discusses the several issues and problems of evaluating financial aid programs and personnel. Sprenkle and Johnson (1976) recommend appropriate administrative tasks for aid administrators and their college presidents.

The administration of federal aid programs on campuses is discussed by Bobowski (1975), Lifsey (1975), and Miller (1975). A report by the Comptroller General of the United States (1974) concludes that there are serious problems with methods used by the federal government to distribute aid among institutions. Hammack (1974) proposes models to predict the way in which federal aid will be distributed among and used by colleges. Morrison and Newman (1975) discuss the organizational structures, policies, and practices of state-supported aid programs.

III.A.1. Adams, F. C. Administering the office of student work and financial assistance. In *Money, marbles, and chalk: Student financial support in higher education*. Keene, R., Adams, F. C., and King, J. E. (Eds.) Carbondale, Ill.: Southern Illinois University Press, 1975.

Discusses the philosophy, goals, and methods of administration of a campus-based aid office.

III.A.2. Aldmon, H. F. Student financial aid administration: A time for action. *Financial Aid Report*, Vol. 1, No. 2, December 1971.

Believes that aid administrators must emphasize new types of activities in the 1970s, including involvement in shaping institutional and national policy.

III.A.3. American College Testing Program. *An annotated bibliography in student financial aid, 1960-1973*. Iowa City, Iowa: American College Testing Program, 1974.

A bibliography of books, articles, dissertations, pamphlets, and brochures on student aid topics.

III.A.4. American College Testing Program. *Handbook for financial aid administrators*. Iowa City, Iowa: American College Testing Program, 1976. (Revised annually)

Provides background information on the financial aid profession; offers suggestions for improvement in management and administration of aid programs; and describes the ACT need analysis services.

III.A.5. Atelsek, F. J. and Gomberg, I. L. *Student assistance: Participants and programs, 1974-75*. Higher Education Panel Report No. 27. Washington, D.C.: American Council on Education, 1975.

Institutional survey on the extent of student participation in United States Office of Education aid programs, characteristics of recipients, student costs, and amounts and sources of aid at colleges and universities. Survey sought suggestions for improvement in administration of the aid programs.

III.A.6. Beck, N. E. and Ryan, D. R. How an institutional aid office really works. In *Perspectives on financial aid*. New York: College Entrance Examination Board, 1975.

Describes the central core of financial aid office activities necessary to meet basic obligations. Offers suggestions for organization, staffing, and administration of campus-based aid offices.

III.A.7. Bekking, J. R. and Stamataros, L. C. Financial aid: Whom should it serve? *Journal of College Student Personnel*, Vol. 13, January 1972, pp. 61-64.

Concerned with the location of the campus aid office in the institutional hierarchy and the executive officer to whom its director should be responsible. Discusses several possibilities and their potential effects.

III.A.8. Bobowski, R. C. Campus-based programs. *American Education*, Vol. 11, November 1975, pp. 29-30.

Brief description of the policies and practices of the federal Supplementary Educational Opportunity Grants (SEOG), National Direct Student Loan (NDSL), and College Work-Study (CWSP) programs.

III.A.9. Bugenhagen, D., et al. *Title IX self-assessment guide for financial aid officers.* Syracuse, N.Y.: Syracuse University, 1976.

A self-assessment guide designed to help financial aid administrators review their policies, practices, and procedures as they relate to Title IX regulations.

III.A.10. Bushnell, V. L. *Analysis of student financial aid programs in four-year colleges and universities.* Tempe, Ariz.: Arizona State University, 1974.

Examines the staffing, office structure, roles of financial aid committees, processes and criteria by which aid is awarded, and relationships of institutional size and location to financial aid practices at western institutions.

III.A.11. Caliendo, N. and Curtice, J. K. Title IX: A guide for financial aid administrators. *Journal of Student Aid,* Vol. 7, May 1977, pp. 32–43.

A self-assessment check list for use by campus aid administrators to evaluate the extent to which their operation of federal aid programs discriminates against men or women.

III.A.12. College Entrance Examination Board. *Perspectives on financial aid: Sources and information.* New York: College Entrance Examination Board, 1975.

Collection of papers on the history, resources, and management of financial aid in the United States.

III.A.13. College Entrance Examination Board. *Report of the Committee on Student Economics.* New York: College Entrance Examination Board, 1972.

Contains committee recommendations on meeting costs of higher education and the roles that parents, students, and governments must be expected to assume.

III.A.14. Comptroller General of the United States. *Administration of the Office of Education's student financial aid programs.* Report to the Special Subcommittee on Education, House Committee on Education and Labor. Washington, D.C.: Government Printing Office, 1974.

Reviews aspects of the Guaranteed Student Loan, National Direct Student Loan, College Work-Study and Supplementary Educational Opportunity Grants programs. The report concludes that the process for allocating loan funds to institutions is not equitable, that some institutions receive more funds than needed while others receive less than needed, and that regional review panels do not have sufficient time or data to effectively act.

III.A.15. College Scholarship Service Student Advisory Committee. *Unmet needs: Report on student financial aid problems from the CSS Student Advisory Committee.* New York: College Entrance Examination Board, 1976.

Reports on a series of hearings in seven states at which students discussed their financial aid problems. Concludes that financial aid system costs are higher for educationally and economically disadvantaged students and that bureaucratic hurdles are greatest for those who have the least experience at surmounting them. Offers specific recommendations to resolve the problems.

III.A.16. College Scholarship Service Student Advisory Committee. What 250 students say about financial aid problems. *College Board Review,* No. 100, Summer 1976, pp. 14–25.

Reports on a series of hearings in seven states at which students discussed their problems with the management and administration of student aid.

III.A.17. Davis, J. S. State student aid program administrator's perceptions of student aid research. *Journal of Student Financial Aid,* Vol. 7, May 1977, pp. 19–25.

Discusses research topics considered important by 36 state program administrators. Reports that, beyond the need for research to support legislative budgetary requests, there is little consensus on the purposes or types of research needed.

III.A.18. De Jarnett, R. P. The organization of student support programs in institutions of higher learning. In *Money, marbles, or chalk: Student financial support in higher education.* Keene, R., Adams, F. C., and King, J. E. (Eds.) Carbondale, Ill.: Southern Illinois University Press, 1975.

Discusses the ideal functional location of the aid office in the university's organizational structure.

III.A.19. Dickson, D. R. Do you believe any of these ten myths about financial aid? *College Board Review,* No. 73, Fall 1969, pp. 14–18.

Lists and debunks ten of the most common myths concerning financial aid, its operation, and its administration.

III.A.20. Donham, D. E. and Stege, L. E. Grants, loans, and scholarships. In *Money, marbles, or chalk: Student financial support in higher education.* Keene, R., Adams, F. C., and King, J. E. (Eds.) Carbondale, Ill.: Southern Illinois University Press, 1975.

Provides an overall view of the types and kinds of financial aid available to students.

III.A.21. Edwards, E. L. and Ingle, J. E. Organizational structure of a financial aid office. In *Perspectives on Financial Aid.* New York: College Entrance Examination Board, 1975.

The authors believe that the financial aid office must be organized in relation to role and functions of the administrator and that aid programs must be designed within the framework of institutional goals and objectives. Discusses the size, staff, budget, work scheduling, and needed resources of a financial aid office.

III.A.22. Elliott, W. F. *Management of admissions and financial aid: The net tuition income concept.* Pittsburgh: University of Pittsburgh, 1974. (Dissertation)

Discusses the use of the net tuition income concept as a management tool. This procedure sets the net revenue produced from the entering freshman class as the objective of the admissions/financial aid process, as opposed to the traditional goal of meeting a specific student quota within a financial aid budget.

III.A.23. Hage, R. K. How well is your financial aid office being run? *College Board Review,* No. 89, Fall 1973, pp. 13-15.

Offers 37 specific recommendations for improving the management and operation of campus-based financial aid programs. Based on experience with a financial aid office evaluation project supported by the Sloan Foundation.

III.A.24. Haines, J. R. Institutional planning: What role for directors of student admissions and financial aid? *Planning for Higher Education,* Vol. 5, August 1976, pp. 3-5.

Argues that, in an era of projected enrollment declines and increased costs, the offices of admissions and student financial aid must assume critical new roles in long-range institutional planning.

III.A.25. Hammack, W. C. *An analysis of the utilization of student financial aid funds at institutions of higher education in the southwest.* Norman, Okla.: University of Oklahoma, 1974. (Dissertation)

Uses federal student aid data from 123 institutions to develop and test models to predict the average amount and type of student aid used by colleges.

III.A.26. Hardesty, W. G., et al. Student participation in forming financial aid policies. *College and University,* Vol. 45, Summer 1970, pp. 415-416.

Panel discussion focusing on the need for minority student input to the financial aid process.

III.A.27. Hartstock, W. W. *A descriptive study of financial aid offices and their operation in institutions of higher education in West Virginia.* Morgantown, W. Va.: West Virginia University, 1974.

Survey of the operation and administration of campus-based aid offices at 23 institutions. Particular attention is given to staffing and training needs.

III.A.28. Hersey, D. M. *A new financial aid policy for Macalester College.* Cambridge, Mass.: Harvard University, 1973. (Dissertation)

Describes the strategies and tactics for developing and implementing a new institutional aid policy.

III.A.29. Huff, R. P. *College admissions and financial aid policies as revealed by institutional practices.* Palo Alto, Calif.: Western Regional Office, College Entrance Examination Board, 1971.

Reviews financial aid policies and their implications for admissions practices at 86 higher education institutions in the nation. Data are analyzed with respect to percentages of applicants seeking aid and receiving aid and the relative composition of aid programs and sources of aid.

III.A.30. Huff, R. P. Institutional financial aid resources. In *Perspectives on financial aid.* New York: College Entrance Examination Board, 1975.

Description of the nature, utilization, and development of institutional financial aid resources.

III.A.31. Jewett, J. E. Proactive planning for admissions: The case of Ohio Wesleyan University. *College and University,* Vol. 51, Spring 1976, pp. 348–359.

Model is employed to estimate applicant enrollments, verbal ability, and need for financial aid.

III.A.32. Keene, R. Evaluation of financial aid personnel and programs. In *Money, marbles, or chalk: Student financial support in higher education.* Keene, R., Adams, F. C., and King, J. E. (Eds.) Carbondale, Ill.: Southern Illinois University Press, 1975.

Discusses problems of financial aid administrators and programs and procedures for evaluating them.

III.A.33. Keene, R., Adams, F. C., and King, J. E. (Eds.) *Money, marbles or chalk: Student financial support in higher education.* Carbondale, Ill.: Southern Illinois University Press, 1975,

A collection of 28 essays on the philosophy, history, development, programs, administration, and operation of student aid.

III.A.34. Kelly, R. N. The new delivery system: A voice for caution. *Journal of Student Financial Aid,* Vol. 7, February 1977, pp. 35–44.

Critique of the recommendations of the National Task Force on Student Aid Problems. Believes those recommendations work to protect the autonomy of institutions by limiting the powers of states and the BEOG program to adjust the aid system to meet their needs.

III.A.35. King, L. J. and Wedemeyer, D. J. Designing an information system for student financial aids. *Journal of Student Financial Aid,* Vol. 4, March 1974, pp. 5–10.

Describes the benefits of management information systems, the resistance to their use, and their implementation. Experience at the University of Hawaii is used as a case study.

III.A.36. Lasko, R. We may not always appear fair, but we most certainly strive to remain legal. *College Board Review,* No. 101, Fall 1976, p. 304.

Believes that the problems students experience because of the management and coordination of financial aid programs will not be alleviated until agreement on more equitable methods of operation is achieved.

III.A.37. Lifsey, R. R. *An analysis of selected categories of federally funded student financial aid at the University of Alabama.* University, Ala.: University of Alabama, 1975. (Dissertation)

Analysis of the legislative basis, administrative regulations, required reports and procedures, and the use of need analysis systems in and for federal programs.

III. A. 38. Lovelace, H., et al. Registrar, admissions, and record offices as seen by the financial aids office. *College and University,* Vol. 51, Summer 1976, pp. 699–705.

Panel discussion on the administrative interaction among these offices at four different institutions. Concludes all three offices should be organized under the same person or post.

III. A. 39. Mace, G. Political considerations for financial aid administrators. In *Money, marbles, or chalk: Student financial support in higher education.* Keene, R., Adams, F. C., and King, J. E. (Eds.) Carbondale, Ill.: Southern Illinois University Press, 1975.

Believes that aid administrators should join forces with student and other groups to gain public support for student aid programs.

III. A. 40. Marmaduke, A. S. The status of student financial aid: An observation. *Journal of Student Financial Aid,* Vol. 4, June 1974, pp. 5–7.

Contends that the current financial aid situation, with its multiplicity of programs, lack of conceptual clarity, and its many managerial problems causes student confusion.

III. A. 41. Miller, G. S. Federal programs. In *Perspectives on financial aid.* New York: College Entrance Examination Board, 1975.

Discusses the major responsibilities of campus-based aid administrators in the administration of federal student aid programs.

III. A. 42. Morrison, D. L. and Newman, D. L. State programs. In *Perspectives on financial aid.* New York: College Entrance Examination Board, 1975.

Discusses the organizational structures, policies, and practices of state grant, loan, and work-study programs. Assesses their impact and future.

III. A. 43. Myers, J. H. Recent federal tax developments affecting colleges, universities, and donors. *Journal of College and University Law,* Vol. 2, Spring 1975, pp. 269–288.

Reviews tax reform bills in Congress as they affect tax status of exempt organizations and tax treatment of scholarships, fellowships, contributions, and bequests.

III. A. 44. Nash, G. Student financial aid, college and university. In *Encyclopedia of educational research.* Ebel, R. L. (Ed.) New York: Macmillan, Inc., 1969.

Provides a brief history of financial aid and a discussion of the growth of federal and state programs. Includes a review of research literature and an extensive bibliography.

III. A. 45. National Task Force on Student Aid Problems. *Final report.* Brookdale, Calif.: National Task Force on Student Aid Problems, 1975.

Discusses the activities, findings, and recommendations of the task force. Includes chapters on the problems of need analysis, aid application forms, coordination and management of aid programs, and the role of students in the student aid system and partnership.

III.A.46. North, W. M. Role and functions of the financial aid officer. In *Perspectives on Financial Aid*. New York: College Entrance Examination Board, 1975.

Believes the role of the aid administrator is dependent on a mutual trust and respect among all persons and agencies concerned with student aid.

III.A.47. North, W. M. The role of the aid officer in the institution. In *Money, marbles, or chalk: Student financial support in higher education*. Keene, R., Adams, F. C., and King, J. E. (Eds.) Carbondale, Ill.: Southern Illinois University Press, 1975.

Discusses the ideal role of the aid officer as defined by duties and tasks and the interests of various parties in student aid. Pays particular attention to the role of the aid officer vis-a-vis other campus administrators.

III.A.48. O'Hearne, J. J. Financial aid office management. *Journal of Student Financial Aid*, Vol. 3, June 1973, pp. 27–33.

Presents suggestions for improving the management of campus-based financial aid offices and program functions.

III.A.49. Pernal, M. And more and more unmet needs. *College Board Review*, No. 101, Fall 1976, p. 4.

Rejoinder to the College Scholarship Service (CSS) Student Advisory Committee's report on student problems with the administration of student aid. Believes many student frustrations are shared by aid administrators and that both are responsible for easing them.

III.A.50. Peterson, D. L. *A study of the accuracy of expected family contributions and school budgets used in processing student financial aid requests in Michigan for the 1971–72 academic year*. East Lansing, Mich.: Michigan State University, 1974. (Dissertation)

Compares expected and actual parental contributions and expected and actual budgets for 634 applicants to state grant programs. Found that expenses were greater than anticipated by the programs and that parental contributions were less. Uses ANOVA technique to determine if any of a number of family personal and financial characteristics influenced the families' ability and willingness to pay educational costs.

III.A.51. Peterson, L., Tatum, J., and Winegar, M. Michigan student financial aid office salary and staffing patterns. *Journal of Student Financial Aid*, Vol. 7, February 1977, pp. 5–15.

Survey of financial aid office salary, staffing, and support conditions at postsecondary institutions in the state. Includes data on vocational schools as well as colleges and universities.

III.A.52. Pletcher, B. P., Moyer, P. E., and Hoffman, J. A. Needed: A year-end resource for financial assistance. *Journal of Student Financial Aid*, Vol. 2, November 1973, pp. 26–33.

Notes the need for additional financial aid resources to help students who desire to attend summer school. Describes a loan program sponsored by a cooperative college, college foundation, and commercial bank lending program to provide these resources at the Medical College of Ohio at Toledo.

III.A.53. Ross, D. M. *1972 legislation and achievements: Pupil personnel, regulation and rights, financial aid, food services, transportation.* Research Brief No. 9. Denver, Colo.: Education Commission of the States, 1973.

A state-by-state compilation of legislative changes relating to certain areas of education.

III.A.54. Sheffield, W., and Meskill, V. P. First aid for recruiting—financial aid. *National Association of College Admissions Counselors Journal,* Vol. 18, November 1973, pp. 13–15.

Believes that financial aid awards should be announced at an earlier date to facilitate student decision-making.

III.A.55. Sprenkle, D. E. and Johnson, R. Do's for financial aid administrators and presidents. *Community and Junior College Journal,* Vol. 47, October 1976, p. 25.

Provides a check list of tasks for financial aid administrators and college presidents to improve the administration of student aid on their campuses.

III.A.56. Tombaugh, R. L. Direct or indirect student aid? *Journal of Student Financial Aid,* Vol. 2, March 1972, pp. 28–34.

Discusses the advantages and disadvantages of providing aid to students through colleges or through a central agency. Believes aid can best be delivered through students' colleges.

III.A.57. U.S. Congress, House Committee on Education and Labor. *Seminars before the Special Subcommittee on Education.* Washington, D.C.: Government Printing Office, 1974.

Report on five informal seminars on financial aid sponsored by the subcommittee in July 1974 to discuss the question "What would be the ideal student financial aid package?"

III.A.58. U.S. Congress, House Committee on Education and Labor. *Student financial assistance (miscellaneous). Hearings before the Special Subcommittee on Education of the Committee on Education and Labor.* Washington, D.C.: Government Printing Office, 1974.

Contains testimony on student assistance. Reviews available aid programs as they relate to current and projected needs and costs of students attending postsecondary institutions.

III.A.59. U.S. Congress, Senate. *Higher education legislation, 1975. Part 1 and Part 2. Hearings before the Sub-Committee on Labor and Public Welfare on oversight and information concerning student assistance under the Higher Education Act.* Washington, D.C.: Government Printing Office, 1975.

Contains nearly 2,000 pages of testimony, documentation, and correspondence concerning all aspects of student assistance under the Higher Education Act of 1972.

III.A.60. Van Dusen, W. D. and O'Hearne, J. J. *A design for a model college financial aid office*. New York: College Entrance Examination Board, 1968. Revised 1973 by W. D. Van Dusen.

Discusses the current types of aid and the principles and practices that guide college financial aid programs. Cites a common core of operational activities on all campuses: counseling about student expenses and aid opportunities, general administration, student motivation and resource development, and research. Discusses how to improve these operations on individual campuses.

III.B. Need Analysis Systems and Issues

The basic purpose of financial aid is to provide assistance to students who would otherwise be unable to participate in postsecondary education or who would not be able to participate in the type or amount of postsecondary education they seek. To determine who qualifies for financial aid, there must be an analysis of financial need. Financial need is determined by deducting from the cost of education the amount that the student and family can reasonably be expected to contribute. The analysis of financial need has produced more thought, research, writing, and emotion than any other issue in financial aid administration.

Hidden within the relatively simple equation for determining need are a variety of complex concepts and debatable issues. On the cost side of the equation are such questions as: What are the legitimate costs of education? Should they include only direct, out-of-pocket costs or should indirect costs such as lost income while attending school be included? Should only student costs be allowed or should some recognition be made of the cost to the family supporting the student or of income lost to the family while the student is in school?

On the contribution side of the equation are issues concerning the most valid and reliable proxies for a student's and family's "real" ability to pay for educational costs? Should ability to pay be assessed against current income, against current income and assets, or against some measure of the future earning potential of both student and parents? How can both horizontal and vertical equity be achieved? What should be done when a family is unwilling or unable to actually contribute what is calculated as reasonable? When does the responsibility shift from the parent and student to the student alone? Should the determination of what is "reasonable" be in any way related to the amount of money available in aid programs to meet need?

The answers to these questions are crucial because they determine who will receive aid, what amounts will be received, and what effects aid will have on student and institutional behavior. The publications in this section are concerned with providing answers to these and other related questions.

Aid administrators, economists, and policymakers first began to develop sophisticated, empirically based answers to these questions in the early 1950s. About this time, the first national need analysis system was developed by the College Scholarship Service (CSS), a voluntary association of colleges and universities (College Scholarship Service, 1976; Henry, 1975). During the next two decades the CSS and many other groups sought answers to the questions and problems of need analysis.

It was not until recently, however, that some degree of consensus was achieved about what constitutes financial need and how that need should be determined. The National Task Force on Student Aid Problems (III. A. 45) helped to achieve this consensus with the development and acceptance of a Uniform Methodology of Need Analysis. The task force further helped to clarify need analysis concepts with a set of definitions:

"Determination of ability to pay is a process which involves the measurement of the economic well-being or financial strength of the candidate and/or his or her family and the subsequent determination of a contribution toward educational expenses through the application of some 'taxation rate' to the measure of financial strength.

"Determination of program eligibility is the translation of the purpose for which a student aid program has been established (whether implicit or explicit) into some measurable indicator of an academic, personal, or financial characteristic of the desired recipient or his or her family.

"Determination of financial need is the measurement of the specific amount of money needed by an individual student attending or planning to attend a particular postsecondary institution." (p. 13)

The Uniform Methodology has been accepted for general use by most state programs, the College Scholarship Service, the American College Testing Program, and most colleges and universities. However, the federal Basic Educational Opportunity Grants Program, some states, and some institutions still use their own need analysis systems. Therefore, the "determination of ability to pay" in need analysis systems is still far from uniform in the administration of financial aid programs. Two references in this section contain some of the rationale and many of the considerations expressed by task force members in the development of the Uniform Methodology (Bowman, 1975; Goggins, 1974). Bowman's (1976) more recent publication presents a lengthy description of the methodology and

Barnes (1977) offers an evaluation and critique of the methodology from an economist's point of view.

Just prior to the creation of the National Task Force on Student Aid Problems, inflation contributed to increasing college costs and decreasing parental ability to pay for them. This caused a great deal of concern among many groups and led to suggestions for revising the College Scholarship Service need analysis system to account for these trends (Huff, 1972–73; Schaeffer, 1973).

While consideration was being given to adjusting family contribution schedules to compensate for inflation, the federal government was concerned that new contribution schedules that increased measured need might result in a demand for aid dollars that could not be met. The government subsequently decided that need analysis systems which were used in the distribution of federal aid dollars should conform to the standards developed internally by the Office of Education. The controversy generated by this decision is discussed in four items (Nelson, 1974–75; Sandler, 1976; U.S. Congress, House Committee on Education and Labor, 1974a; U.S. Congress, Senate Committee on Labor and Public Welfare, 1974, 1975).

There have been other, earlier proposals for modifying need analysis systems. Kaminsky (1973) proposed that parental contributions be adjusted for regional cost-of-living differences. Johnstone (1973) and Jones (1973) were both critical of the treatment of family assets in need analysis systems and offered suggestions for improvement. Pyrdol (1974) suggested a new way of treating social security benefits. Robbins (1972) asserted that economic measurements of students' work-debt potential should be used in need analysis and Erickson (1972) briefly described the present-value-total-resources approach to need analysis which was considered by The College Board's Panel on Student Need Analysis (II.B.2). More recently, Horch (1976) conducted a study to determine if stepwise regression analysis could be used to simplify need analysis.

Two documents published early in the 1970s provide helpful information on the theory and practices of need analysis and their effects on the distribution of financial aid. Orwig (1971) traces the historical development of the concept of financial need and the procedures used to measure it. He describes the relationship of need analysis to available aid, the problems in choosing appropriate standards of living in need analysis measurement, the effects of changing economic conditions on parental ability to pay for education. Orwig and Jones (1970) test the utility of a number of financial variables in predicting parental contributions to educational expenses. They conclude that the best predictors of parental contributions are parents' federal income tax returns and nontaxable income, investments and net value of farm, business, and real estate holdings, and home equity and savings.

Two dissertations (Kunz, 1970; Orwig, 1970) on the use of need analysis systems by different colleges and universities explain why it has been difficult to obtain consensus in need analysis practices and procedures. These studies show that aid administrators on different campuses have very specific, if sometimes idiosyncratic, reasons for preferring one need analysis system over another. Preferences are frequently related to how different financial variables are treated, how the use of a given system results in distribution of aid to the students the institutions most (or least) want to assist, and what philosophic beliefs administrators hold regarding how much parents should pay for their children's education.

Regardless of which system of need analysis is used by a program, researchers agree that individual results of analysis should be carefully examined by professional aid administrators. Cogent statements on this need are offered by Hage (1974), Gambee (1974), and Van Dusen and Cavanaugh (1977).

The validity of information presented by students and parents on need analysis documents is a concern of most aid programs. Eight documents in this section are concerned with assessing the validity and reliability of this data. While consensus on how student and family data should be treated in need analysis systems has not been achieved, it is almost universally accepted that the data themselves should be as accurate as possible.

Studies of the reliability of financial aid data have produced mixed results. For example, Anderson (1974), Curtis (1972), Collins (1973), and Rutter and Wickstrom (1976) believe that the validity of need analysis data must be verified by other documents, primarily Internal Revenue Service tax forms. However, Bowman (1974–75, 1974) indicates that determination of need analysis from tax form data would produce only limited redistribution of aid funds as need analysis data are generally quite valid. Diegnau and Van Dusen (1975) and Schonhart (1975) find overestimates and underestimates of income and income-related data from some groups, but also find that most groups present accurate information. Establishing the validity of need analysis data is an important issue, but the degree to which invalid data is a problem or the extent to which programs should go to assure validity has not yet been established.

In all need analysis systems, the key factor is the determination of *ability*, rather than *willingness*, to pay for educational costs. Nelson (1974) finds that parents contributed about 95 percent of the mean expected amounts necessary to meet their children's educational costs. Pierog (1976), with a much smaller sample, concludes that children from low-income families are more likely than those from high-income families to receive the *expected* amounts of parental contributions.

III. B. 1. Anderson, J. E. *The reliability of information reported on the* ACT *comprehensive financial aid report by financial aid applicants at the University of Northern Colorado.* Greeley, Colo.: University of Northern Colorado, 1974.

Compared responses to IRS tax form data. Found no significant differences in the reported income and number of exemptions claimed, but found significant differences in reported income tax paid, computed parental contributions, and student financial aid.

III. B. 2. Barnes, G. T. An economist's approach to reforming the uniform methodology. *Journal of Student Financial Aid,* Vol. 7, May 1977, pp. 10–18.

Evaluates the National Task Force on Student Aid Problem's uniform methodology for determining student financial need. Believes that it fails to treat income and assets in a consistent manner and, consequently, favors parents who are homeowners, well-educated, widowed or divorced, and who own wealth in forms other than stocks, bonds, bank accounts, or real estate.

III. B. 3. Bowman, J. L. *Accuracy of parents' taxable income reports for the 1972–73 processing year.* Princeton, N.J.: College Scholarship Service of the College Entrance Examination Board, 1974.

Compares the reports of 2,000 families to the CSS and the Internal Revenue Service. Comparisons included: tax filing status, numbers of dependents, income from wages and other sources, business expenses, federal income tax paid, expected parental contributions, and filing dates. Reveals that data on both forms were generally similar and that use of "validated" data from IRS forms in need analysis would result in relatively small redistributions of aid among applicants.

III. B. 4. Bowman, J. L. *A uniform methodology for measuring ability to pay: The* CSS *national standard.* Princeton, N.J.: College Scholarship Service of the College Entrance Examination Board, 1975.

Describes the underlying assumptions and the treatment of student and family financial data in the CSS need analysis system for 1975–76.

III. B. 5. Bowman, J. L. *Measuring student resources for postsecondary educational expenses.* New York: College Entrance Examination Board, 1975.

Reviews the current treatment of student resources in the CSS need analysis system. Suggests increased amounts of expected student contributions from summer earnings and proposes that students' social security benefits be treated as family income rather than as student resources.

III. B. 6. Bowman, J. L. *On the determination of effective income in* CSS *needs analysis procedures.* Princeton, N.J.: College Scholarship Service, 1969.

Analyzes the "effective income" concept then being used in the CSS need analysis system and proposes changes in the allowance structure.

III.B.7. Bowman, J. L. Parents' reports of income—How accurate are they? *College Board Review,* No. 94, Winter 1974–75, pp. 9–13.

Compares financial statements reported on the Parents' Confidential Statement (PCS) with those on IRS tax forms. The study found that more than three-fourths of the families reported the same income on both forms, that reports of wage and salary earners are more accurate than those of families with incomes from other sources, that correspondence was greater when the tax form was filed first, and that use of tax form data rather than PCS data would result only in small redistributions of aid funds among students.

III.B.8. Bowman, J. L. *The uniform methodology revisited: A review of the dependent and independent student models.* Princeton, N.J.: College Scholarship Service of the College Entrance Examination Board, 1976.

Reviews the CSS standard for 1975–76 in view of comments and concerns of CSS users and the Office of Education's rules regarding the annual review of need analysis systems. Describes some areas which are topics of revision in the standard, including treatment of assets, of social security benefits, and of families with more than one member attending postsecondary institutions.

III.B.9. Bowman, J. L. and Horch, D. H. *Measuring the financial status of graduate and professional students.* Princeton, N.J.: Graduate and Professional School Financial Aid Service, 1975. (Revised annually)

Sets forth the rationale for estimating students' and parents' ability to contribute toward the cost of graduate and professional school which is implemented in the need analysis services of the Graduate and Professional School Financial Aid Service. Discusses treatment of student and parental resources and assets, summer savings expectations, social security benefits, and tax and retirement allowances.

III.B.10. Bowman, J. L. and Weiss, G. S. *Measuring the financial strength of family assets.* Princeton, N.J.: College Scholarship Service, 1970.

Reviews the treatment of family assets in the CSS need analysis system and recommends changes in light of changing economic conditions. Issues discussed include protection of assets for retirement, conversion of discretionary net worth to effective income, and treatment of home equity.

III.B.11. Bowman, J. L. and Weiss, G. S. *Place to place differences in the cost of living.* Princeton, N.J.: College Scholarship Service of the College Entrance Examination Board, 1967.

Discusses the use of indexes for place to place differences in costs of living in a national need analysis system. Two of the more difficult problems identified are lack of good data and the inability to limit the comparisons to costs independent of differences in income levels.

III. B. 12. College Scholarship Service. CSS *Need Analysis: Theory and computation procedures for the 1977–78 PCS and SFS including sample cases and tables.* New York: College Entrance Examination Board, 1976. (Revised annually)

Guide to the general administration of aid programs and use of the CSS need analysis system. Discusses principles and practices of aid administration, history and theory of need analysis, computation procedures for need analysis documents, and construction of student expense budgets.

III. B. 13. College Scholarship Service. *Learning to use the CSS need analysis system.* New York: College Entrance Examination Board, 1976.

One-hour course supported by tape cassettes designed to teach aid administrators how to use the CSS need analysis system.

III. B. 14. Collins, J. S. Verification of parental income estimates by means of federal tax returns – The experience at one institution. *Journal of Student Financial Aid,* Vol. 3, November 1973, pp. 20–25.

Data collected at Boston College indicated that parental underestimates of income on need analysis documents are a serious problem, especially for middle-income parents. Believes copies of tax returns should be used to verify need analysis statements.

III. B. 15. Cunningham, J. P. Estimating parents' income in succeeding year – Accuracy of present CSS system. *Journal of Student Financial Aid,* Vol. 2, May 1972, pp. 8–12.

Compares parental estimates of income to actual income for those filing Parents' Confidential Statements at Wesleyan University in 1970. Suggests that the College Scholarship Service (CSS) use a prediction factor based on least-squares parameters to make a more accurate estimate of parents' income in succeeding years.

III. B. 16. Curtis, G. E. Emancipation, divorce, separation, dependency: Who should provide family financial information? *Journal of Student Financial Aid,* Vol. 5, May 1975, pp. 40–45.

Discusses the problems of analyzing the financial needs of applicants from "atypical" families and recommends full disclosure of potential resources from all aid applicants.

III. B. 17. Curtis, G. E. How reliable is PCS information? The case for collection of analysis of tax returns. *Journal of Student Financial Aid,* Vol. 2, November 1972, pp. 18–22.

Because parents underestimate their income on PCS documents and the CSS is responsible for verification of PCS data, the author recommends that the CSS collect tax returns and verify data for its users.

III. B. 18. Dent, R. A. Student resources. In *Perspectives on financial aid.* New York: College Entrance Examination Board, 1975.

Discusses amounts and types of self-help resources available to and expected from students in payment of educational costs.

III. B. 19. Diegnau, S. I. and Van Dusen, W. D. Another look at income verification. *Journal of Student Financial Aid,* Vol. 5, November 1975, pp. 3-14.

Reports on a study comparing information from income tax returns to data on the PCS submitted at California State University at Long Beach. Although the study found that the majority of parents provide accurate information, the authors suggest that verification of data is still important.

III. B. 20. Erickson, E. W. Present-value-total-resources and horizontal equity. *Financial Aid Report,* Vol. 1, May 1972.

Provides a general description of the present-value-total-resources concept and its relationship to financial need analysis.

III. B. 21. Gambee, S. Exercising judgment and making exceptions. *Financial Aid Report,* Vol. 3, June 1974.

Discusses guidelines for the financial aid administrator's exercise of judgment in the administration of federal aid programs.

III. B. 22. Goggins, W. S. *The measurement of economic well-being in need analysis models.* ACT Research Report No. 66. Iowa City, Iowa: American College Testing Program, 1974.

Describes current practices for the measurement of student and parental ability to pay for college. Discusses their economic weaknesses and proposes a two-step model for evaluating them. The first step is to compare their theoretical implications; the second is to compare them for implications in perceived distribution of well-being among all applicant families.

III. B. 23. Hage, R. K. Twenty-two reasons for reviewing the FNAR. *Financial Aid Report,* Vol. 3, January, 1974.

Describes 22 cases at Dartmouth College for which the CSS financial need analysis report was reviewed and adjusted as examples of the need for such professional review and exercise of judgment.

III. B. 24. Henry, J. B. Student financial aid analysis. In *Money, marbles, or chalk: Student financial support in higher education.* Keene, R., Adams, F. C., and King, J. E. (Eds.) Carbondale, Ill.: Southern Illinois University Press, 1975.

Discusses the historical evolution and major concepts of need analysis as well as current issues and future trends.

III. B. 25. Horch, D. H. Can need analysis procedure be simplified through stepwise regression analyses? *Journal of Student Financial Aid,* Vol. 6, November 1976, pp. 22-32.

Uses data on PCS filers in 1973-74 to demonstrate that stepwise regression analysis does not hold much promise as a technique for simplifying need analysis.

III. B. 26. Horch, D. H. Measuring the ability of undergraduate married students to contribute to educational costs. *Journal of Student Financial Aid,* Vol. 3, November 1973, pp. 34-43.

By considering married students' financial need in two parts (aid required to meet the students' maintenance and direct educational costs and aid required to meet their families' maintenance costs), a need analysis procedure can be developed to measure need for grant subsidies that is comparable to that used for unmarried students.

III. B. 27. Huff, R. P. css need assessment of upper-middle income families – Are they being excluded? *College Board Review,* No. 86, Winter 1972–73, p. 25.

Maintains that a new css need analysis formula needs to be devised to allow students from above average income families to attend private colleges without too great a financial burden.

III. B. 28. Jackson, L. M. *Financial aid: Who needs it?* MIS Research Profile. Washington, D.C.: Institute for Services to Education, Inc., 1973.

Describes differences between the css and ACT need analysis systems in determining who has financial need and discusses which service would be more appropriately used by applicants to predominantly black colleges.

III. B. 29. Johnstone, D. B. Beyond need analysis. *College Board Review,* No. 87, Spring 1973, pp. 13–15.

Forecasts significant changes in financial aid administration. Believes that financial aid will increasingly flow directly to students independent of their institutions or their financial aid offices. Financial aid officers will become general financial counselors to both students and colleges. They will use need analysis as a tool, but will also have means of estimating student demands for education, future earnings potential, tolerable debt levels, and the costs to students of time spent outside the labor market.

III. B. 30. Johnstone, D. B. Liquidity of assets in determining expected parental contributions. *Financial Aid Report,* Vol. 3, September 1973.

Believes that taxing "illiquid" family assets in need analysis systems may place a heavy strain on use of current cash income and on liquid assets.

III. B. 31. Jones, J. S. Some thoughts on the css treatment of family assets. *Journal of Student Financial Aid,* Vol. 3, June 1973, pp. 4–11.

Believes the current css treatment of family assets is too sophisticated, too complicated, and contains too many dilemmas, paradoxes, and anomalies. Suggests several ways to alleviate these conditions.

III. B. 32. Kaminsky, R. Adjusting the parental contribution for regional cost-of-living differences. *Financial Aid Report,* Vol. 3, September 1973.

Recommends that the css need analysis system provide aid administrators with a procedure for adjusting parental contributions on the basis of cost-of-living differences.

III. B. 33. Kunz, W. N. *A study of institutions' own methods of student financial need analysis.* Buffalo, N.Y.: State University of New York at Buffalo, 1970. (Dissertation)

Examines need analysis methods of 207 colleges that participate in federal aid programs. Study revealed a wide range of differences in expected contributions from similar families at different institutions. Also describes why institutions use their own methods.

III. B. 34. Nelson, J. E. Are parents expected to pay too much? *College Board Review*, No. 92, Summer 1974, pp. 11-15.

Analyzes data from state and institutional Student Resource Surveys in 1972-73, reveals that parents were contributing slightly over half the mean amounts *expected* by PCS need analysis. But parents were contributing about 95 percent of the mean expected amounts *necessary* to meet student costs at various institutions. Therefore, the CSS standards reasonably represent the central pattern of actual parental contributions.

III. B. 35. Nelson, J. E. Measuring need versus meeting need. *College Board Review*, No. 94, Winter 1974-1975, pp. 14-17.

Defends changes in the CSS need analysis system which reflect economic difficulties due to inflation and presents a strong case for the determination of financial need without consideration of the amounts of aid available to meet that need.

III. B. 36. Orwig, M. D. *A survey of financial need analysis methods used in institutions of higher education.* Bloomington, Ind.: Indiana University, 1970. (Dissertation)

Analyzes the distribution of need analysis systems at institutions, the attitudes of aid administrators toward them, and the procedures preferred by most administrators.

III. B. 37. Orwig, M. D. *Toward more equitable distribution of college student aid funds: Problems in assessing student financial need.* Iowa City, Iowa: American College Testing Program, 1971.

Traces the development of the concept of financial need and examines various procedures used to measure it. Discusses the relationship of need analysis to aggregate available aid, the choice of appropriate living standards in need analysis, different effects of absolute and relative need, and the effects of changing economic conditions on parental ability to pay for education.

III. B. 38. Orwig, N. D. and Jones, P. K. *Can financial need analysis be simplified?* ACT Research Report No. 33. Iowa City, Iowa: American College Testing Program, 1970.

Reports on problems of collecting financial data on aid applicants. Indicates that best predictors of parents' expected contributions are the federal income tax paid by parents, nontaxable income, investments, the net value of a farm, business, or real estate, home equity, and savings.

III. B. 39. Pierog, J. J. *A comparison study of the actual and expected parental contribution, as a student financial resource, for high and low income students.* Fort Lauderdale, Fla.: Nova University, 1976. (Dissertation)

Study to determine if students actually receive the parental support presupposed in establishing their need. Less than one-third of the high-income students received at least 80 percent of the expected family contribution. Over 87 percent of the low-income students received at least 80 percent of the expected contribution.

III. B. 40. Pyrdol, J. W. A closer look at social security benefits. *Financial Aid Report,* Vol. 3, June 1974.

Discusses the problems of need analysis of students receiving social security benefits and proposes solutions.

III. B. 41. Robbins, H. A. Measuring a student's work-debt potential. *Financial Aid Report,* Vol. 1, May 1972.

Suggests that college expenses are an investment on which students expect returns and, therefore, an economic measure of the students' work-debt potential should be developed and used in conjunction with need analysis.

III. B. 42. Rutter, T. M. and Wickstrom, N. The use of income tax returns in the needs analysis procedure. *Journal of Student Financial Aid,* Vol. 6, February 1976, pp. 15-19.

Describes the efforts of the University of California at San Diego, to systemize and develop useful evaluation formulas for verifying income through use of data obtained from federal income tax returns.

III. B. 43. Sandler, B. S. One cheer for OE. *College Board Review,* No. 101, Fall 1976, pp. 16-19.

Observations on the reactions to and potential effects of regulations requiring that need analysis formulas used to award aid from federal programs must be approved by the Office of Education. The author believes the intervention is not all bad.

III. B. 44. Schaeffer, W. P. College costs versus middle incomes — A proposal. *Journal of Student Financial Aid,* Vol. 3, June 1973, pp. 38-48.

Believes that the CSS need analysis system should redefine its "moderate income level" standard to vary with family income and rewrite tables for taxing discretionary income to help more middle-income families qualify for financial assistance.

III. B. 45. Schonart, P. T. A comparison of reported incomes: BEOG versus PCS. *Journal of Student Financial Aid,* Vol. 5, May 1975, pp. 34-39.

Compares estimates of 1973 gross income reported by the parents of students attending the State University of New York College at Fredonia. Comparison revealed patterns of overestimates and underestimates among different groups of students.

III. B. 46. Sharon, A. T. and Horch, D. H. Accuracy in estimating parents' contributions to students' college expenses. *Journal of College Student Personnel,* Vol. 13, September 1972, pp. 448-451.

Uses data from CSS's Parents' Confidential Statements to analyze whether parents at different income levels are equally accurate in estimating future income and to compare the accuracy of three different methods of estimating income and parents' contributions. Found that methods of estimating future income consistently overestimated the future income of low-income families.

III.B.47. U.S. Congress, House Committee on Education and Labor. *Basic opportunity grants family contribution schedule – 1975-76. Hearings before the Special Subcommittee on Education of the Committee on Education and Labor.* Washington, D.C.: Government Printing Office, 1974a.

Testimony and supporting evidence are provided on the Basic Educational Opportunity Grants (BEOG) contribution schedule of 1975-76.

III.B.48. U.S. Congress, House Committee on Education and Labor. *Student financial aid, Part 1, Theory and practice of need analysis.* Washington, D.C.: Government Printing Office, 1974b.

Testimony on the theory and practice of need analysis, especially as it applies to the administration of federal student aid programs.

III.B.49. U.S. Congress, House Committee on Education and Labor. *Student need analysis (Budgetary concerns or ability to pay?). Oversight hearing before the Subcommittee on Postsecondary Education of the Committee on Education and Labor.* Washington, D.C.: Government Printing Office, 1975.

Hearings held to receive public comments about the Commission of Education's treatment of new need analysis formulas developed by the CSS and ACT.

III.B.50. U.S. Congress, Senate Committee on Labor and Public Welfare. *Second session on the examination of the family contribution schedule for the Basic Educational Opportunity Grant Program for use in academic year 1975-76.* Washington, D.C.: Government Printing Office, 1974.

Testimony and supporting evidence are provided on the BEOG contribution schedule for 1975-76.

III.B.51. U.S. Congress, Senate Committee on Labor and Public Welfare. *Family contribution schedule for the Basic Educational Opportunity Grant Program, 1975.* Hearing before the Subcommittee on Education. Washington, D.C.: Government Printing Office, 1975.

Examination of the 1976-77 family contribution schedule proposed by the Office of Education. Topics discussed were treatment of assets reserves, farm and business assets, and family size offsets.

III.B.52. Van Dusen, W. D. and Cavanaugh, W. J. Goin' through changes: A study of institutional adjustments to central need analysis. *Journal of Student Financial Aid*, Vol. 7, February 1977, pp. 25-33.

Reports on a field test at nine California colleges conducted by the CSS Institutional Verification and Adjustment Service. Describes the kinds of changes aid officers made on PCS need analysis statements, noting that the changes would have produced more equity in the distribution of aid among applicants and reduced the total amount of aid awarded.

III.C. Student Expenses and Expense Budgets

The cost of education is a critical factor in a student's decision to attend or continue an educational program. Determination of this cost also plays an important role in need analysis. The cost of education, the so-called student expense budget, is the amount from which expected family contributions are subtracted to determine financial need.

The extent to which student expense budgets reflect real student costs will have a great impact on the distribution of available aid resources among various groups of students. If the budgets used in need analysis are larger than the amounts students typically spend, then financial aid funds used to meet needs will be underutilized. That is, some students will receive more aid than necessary, potentially denying aid to other students.

On the other hand, if expense budgets are lower than amounts typically spent by students, then the aid they may receive cannot meet their financial needs, thereby reducing the real effects of aid on student access, choice, and retention. Furthermore, when unrealistic budgets are presented to prospective students, the students are misled as to the true costs of their education, thereby reducing their ability to plan to meet the real costs.

In spite of the obvious importance of accurately assessing student costs of education for need analysis and student planning purposes, this issue has received little attention in the literature of financial aid. Fewer than 20 items in this bibliography are solely related to assessment or discussion of costs. (Studies and surveys are listed in Section VII. G.) Some of the issues involved in the construction of student expense budgets include: (1) what kinds of expenses (for example, transportation costs, personal expenditures, medical and dental expenses, child care costs, education loan repayments) should be included in budgets; (2) determination of appropriate classifications of student expense budget groups (for example, budgets for on-campus and off-campus, married and single, undergraduate and graduate, or full-time and part-time students); and (3) determination of reasonable amounts of expenditures for various expense items. In this last area, there are questions concerning whether expense budget standards should be based on expenditure patterns of all students or just financial aid recipients.

The National Task Force on Student Aid Problems (III. A. 45) focused attention on these issues and created increased interest in their resolution. The task force recommended that student budgets "be developed, constructed, and presented to students in a manner which will reflect the types and amounts of expenditures that students within budgetary types experience in maintaining a moderate but adequate standard of living" (p.28).

The task force further recommended that federal and state governments, along with need analysis services and aid administrators' professional associations, should help institutions conduct research to develop more valid student expense budgets.

Two cited here were prompted by task force activities and efforts. One is a collection of papers on student budgets and research from a conference held by the Midwest Association of Student Financial Aid Administrators and the United States Office of Education (1976). The second (Sprenkle, 1976) elaborates on the concern of the task force and other agents for development of appropriate student expense budgets.

One of the more attractive means of collecting data for student expense budgets is through use of student expense diaries. This practice involves asking various groups of students to keep daily and weekly records of their expenditures for various kinds of items. Two articles describe this method and its use (Bowman, 1975 and McKinley and Ramaswany, 1971). Goldberg and Anderson (1975) discuss the relationship between increased budgetary costs and increasing family incomes.

III.C.1. Bowman, W. W. Keeping up with student expenses: Toward systematic methods of computing student budgets. *Journal of Student Financial Aid,* Vol. 5, May 1975, pp. 12-24.

Describes a small pilot study at the University of California at Berkeley to test the use of student expenditure diaries to verify financial aid budgets.

III.C.2. Goldberg, D. and Anderson, A. Average family may spend one-third of its income on college. *Intellect,* Vol. 104, December 1975, p. 214.

Very brief summary of studies conducted at the University of Michigan indicating that a family with a median income of $13,000 would have to pay about one-third of its income to put two children through one year of college.

III.C.3. McKinley, R. J. and Ramaswany, P. *The feasibility of collecting student expenditure and income data by diary methods.* Urbana, Ill.: Student Research Laboratory, University of Illinois, 1971.

An analysis of the problems and practices of collecting student budget information through the use of student diaries.

III.C.4. Midwest Association of Student Financial Aid Administrators/United States Office of Education. *Invitational student expense budget conference working papers.* Evanston, Ill.: Midwest Association of Student Financial Aid Administrators, 1976. (Mimeographed)

Collection of papers on student budget policies, development of student budgets, and methods of research on students' costs of education.

III.C.5. Sprenkle, D. E. Student expense budgets. *Community and Junior College Journal,* Vol. 47, October 1976, pp. 18-23.

Discusses concern expressed by colleges, aid programs, and members of the National Task Force on Student Aid Problems on the appropriate development of student expense budgets.

III.D. Student Aid Counseling and Information Services

Providing information and guidance to students and their families is one of the most important activities of financial aid program management. Most frequently this information and guidance concern the costs of education, ways and means of budgeting expenses, determination of financial need, and availability of aid resources to meet needs.

Without accurate and timely data on the costs of education and available aid resources, students and parents cannot effectively or efficiently plan and pay for the costs of education. Without advice on budgeting, the aid resources and the student's own and his family's resources are less likely to be effectively used to pay for expenses. In addition to these kinds of data, students must also receive information on the terms of some types of aid; for example, how loans must be repaid or what work is required for work-study awards.

Getting accurate, comprehensible, and timely information to students and parents is a vital and difficult task. Two items in this section report on national projects on information dissemination (College Scholarship Service, 1977; National Student Educational Fund, 1976). Both reports provide excellent overviews of the issues and problems of getting financial aid and related data to students. Moore (1973) describes how much and how little parents know about financial aid and El-Khawas (1975) discusses the need for better information dissemination in connection with new consumer-rights legislation.

Six of the following items contain specific suggestions for getting information to students (Bannister and Griswold, 1974; Bob and Davis, 1976; Centore, 1975; Trutko, 1976; Von Klein) et al., 1976; Whalen, 1975. O'Hearne (1975) provides a booklet designed to help counselors get aid information to students and parents.

Four references describe and discuss the role and function of the financial aid counselor. Bowman (1975), Fields (1974), and Quesada-Fulgado (1974) all assert the importance of counseling and the student personnel point of view in financial aid. Polakoff (1972) presents a case study of the role of aid counselors in urban colleges.

Harris (1968) advocates the need for financial aid administrators to devote special counseling efforts to minority/poverty students. Bellia (1971) further illustrates this need by describing a study in which minority students were less likely than white students to have positive feelings about their relationships with aid administrators.

III. D. 1. Bannister, J. C. and Griswold, A. M. Group interviews: An effective approach to counseling students concerning loan responsibilities. *Journal of Student Financial Aid,* Vol. 4, March 1974, pp. 34–39.
Discusses the experiences of group counseling at Memphis State University.

III. D. 2. Bellia, A. J. Variations in the response of black and white students in their relationship with the financial aid counselor. *Journal of Student Financial Aid,* Vol. 1, November 1971, pp. 41–46.
Summarizes research at Canisius College (New York) on the relationship between students and financial aid counselors. Found that black students felt less positive about their relationships than white students. Offers some suggestions for improving financial aid counseling.

III. D. 3. Bob, S. and Davis, H. Student financial aid: A community service. *Community and Junior College Journal,* Vol. 47, October 1976, pp. 26–27.
Describes the results of 30 high school and community financial aid dissemination workshops. The workshops were held in 1975–76 by Montgomery Community College.

III. D. 4. Bowman, A. E. The financial aid counselor – A true educator. In *Money, marbles, or chalk: Student financial support in higher education.* Keene, R., Adams, F. C., and King, J. E. (Eds.) Carbondale, Ill.: Southern Illinois University Press, 1975.
Believes that aid administrators must use guidance and counseling skills in working with students and their families.

III. D. 5. Centore, A. R. *Financial aid specialist in the secondary school.* Paper presented at the annual meeting of the American Personnel and Guidance Association, March 1975. (ERIC: ED 110894; CG 011021)
Outlines several programs instituted at one high school in an effort to disseminate financial aid information to students.

III. D. 6. College Scholarship Service. *Making it count: A project to provide better information about costs and financial aid to students making postsecondary choices.* New York: College Entrance Examination Board, 1977.
Discusses the need for better financial aid information and the problems of getting it to students; describes the results of a survey on what students say they need to know; and offers some recommendations for improving the process. Contains brief descriptions of the information-dissemination efforts of several institutions.

III. D. 7. El-Khawas, E. Consumerism as an emerging issue for postsecondary education. *Educational Record,* Vol. 56, Spring 1975, pp. 126–131.
Describes steps institutions can take to avoid increased federal regulations by

complying with consumer standards of truth-in-advertising and full disclosure of information to students.

III. D. 8. Fields, C. R. Financial aid officer: Accountant or counselor? *Journal of Student Financial Aid,* Vol. 4, June 1974, pp. 8-14.

Counseling as an essential function of financial aid administration is described in terms of opportunities, goals, problems, and responsibilities.

III. D. 9. Harris, J. W. New role for the student aid officer: Resourceful uncle. *College Board Review,* No. 67, Spring 1968, pp. 24-26.

Describes the college adjustment and adaptation problems of minority/poverty students and offers some suggestions on how the aid administrator can and should help to alleviate them.

III. D. 10. Moore, D. R. Student financial aid: How much do parents know? *Journal of the National Association of Student Personnel Administrators,* Vol. 10, 1973, pp. 232-237.

Survey of parent participants at "financial aid nights" in New York revealed that only one-fourth of the parents had received aid information from guidance counselors and that most had made no plans for paying for college expenses. Stresses the need for aid administrators to provide parents with better information.

III. D. 11. National Student Education Fund. *The options handbook: Communicating with prospective students about postsecondary educational options: Summary and recommendations.* Washington, D.C.: National Student Educational Fund, 1976.

Final report on the Student Information Gap Project for 1974-75. The project was a student analysis of the inadequate amount, quality, form, and sources of information available to postsecondary students and prospective students about programs and institutions of education. Contains a series of recommendations on consumer protection, student rights, the administration of student aid, and counseling.

III. D. 12. O'Hearne, J. J. *Counselors and financial aid: Helping students plan for college.* New York: College Entrance Examination Board, 1975.

Booklet to assist counselors in answering students' and parents' questions about paying for college. Discusses educational expenses, budgeting, need analysis, and the various types of aid.

III. D. 13. Polakoff, S. E. *The role of the financial aid counselor in an urban college setting.* New York: Columbia University, 1972. (Dissertation)

Describes the role of the financial aid counselor with particular emphasis on counselor response to nonfinancial student problems. Based on analysis of the activities of six counselors in two public urban colleges.

III. D. 14. Quesada-Fulgado, C. The role of counseling in financial aid. *Journal of Student Financial Aid,* Vol. 4, March 1974, pp. 19-24.

Because the financial need of students is determined by their educational and vocational plans, career goals, and personal growth and development, the author believes that the financial aid program should be a part of campus student personnel services and operate within a counseling frame of reference.

III.D.15. Trutko, H. M. Financial aid information: Does your message get lost? *Journal of Student Financial Aid,* Vol. 6, February 1976, pp. 11–14.

Describes some practices which financial aid administrators and high school guidance counselors can use to better provide students and parents with financial aid information.

III.D.16. Von Klein, W., et al. Marketing student financial aid. *College and University,* Vol. 51, Summer 1976, pp. 757–763.

Report on a panel discussion on providing students with financial aid information and dollars. Describes several approaches to information dissemination.

III.D.17. Whalen, C. The high school relations aspects of financial aid. *Journal of Student Financial Aid,* Vol. 5, November 1975, pp. 21–26.

Discusses the problems and goals of dissemination of financial aid information in high schools. Emphasizes simplification and clarification of information given by colleges to high school students and counselors.

III.E. Packaging Aid Awards

Packaging aid awards refers to the process in which different types and amounts of aid are combined to form a total aid package to a single student. For example, one student's aid package might total $1,500 — $500 in a grant, $500 in a loan, and $500 in an employment or work-study award. Another student's aid package might total $1,500, but be comprised of $1,000 in grant money and $500 in a loan. To further illustrate the packaging process and concept, $500 in grant money to each student may come from a state-supported program but an additional $500 in grant money to the latter student may come from institutional sources.

Packaging is usually performed by institutional aid administrators who take into account each student's aid from outside sources (for example, Basic Educational Opportunity Grants, state scholarship or grant awards, or educational benefits) and then round out the student's aid package with awards from funds they control. In ideal cases, the total aid package will fully meet the student's financial need.

Packaging as a process is important because through it inequities of the student aid system can potentially be corrected. For example, suppose two students have equal financial aid needs of $1,000. The first student has been awarded a state grant of $500, but the second has received only a $200 grant from some outside source. The institutional aid administrator may choose to award the first student a $500 loan to complete his aid package and award the second student a $300 institutional grant *and* a $500 loan to complete his package. Both students' aid packages would thereby be made equal, each receiving an equal amount of grant and loan money.

The underlying packaging philosophy here is that students with equal financial needs should receive equal types and amounts of aid to meet their needs. The types of aid received are frequently as significant as the amounts because some aid (for example, loans and work awards) requires student repayment in dollars or service. It is generally believed that two students with equal needs and financial circumstances should receive equal amounts of aid which do not require repayment (grants, scholarships, and education benefits) and types of aid which do require repayment.

The present financial aid system creates situations in which some students receive more aid than others. The aid administrator can package aid to help alleviate these inequities. As the National Task Force on Student Aid Problems (III. A. 45) noted: "packaging is the moment of truth when it all comes together, where the broad funnel of aid resources comes to its narrowest point and those resources are delivered to the student" (p. 68). At this point, the aid administrator can balance the kinds and amounts of total aid received by different students.

Although the process and impact of packaging is quite important, it has received little attention in the literature of financial aid. The CSS Panel on Student Financial Need Analysis (II. B. 2) studied the types of awards received by different types of students. Schlekat (VII. A. 31) discovered that lower-income students were more likely than middle-income students to receive less valuable types of awards — that is, loans and work awards — in their aid packages. Aside from these two efforts, the task force's report, and the two items listed below, very little on this topic will be found in the literature.

There is a need for more articulation of the philosophies of packaging. There is perhaps a greater need for more empirical research on the effects of various types and amounts of aid packages on student access, choice, and retention. Some evidence of this impact can be garnered, with effort, from studies on the impact of financial aid in general (see Section VII, A through D), but much more data are needed. As long as the current inequities in the distribution of aid exist, more evidence on their effects and the alleviating effects of aid packaging will be needed.

III. E. 1. Bingham, R. G. Financial aid packaging: Student serving or institution serving? *National Association of College Admissions Counselors Journal,* Vol. 15, August 1970, pp. 23–25.

Argues that aid packaging should be based on parental incomes rather than past student achievement.

III.E.2. Brown, R. M. *Equity packaging of student financial aid.* New York: College Entrance Examination Board, 1976.

Believes that packaging of aid should reflect national and institutional philosophy about who should have access to college, who should pay, and how applicants can be treated equitably. Describes the "equity packaging" system recommended by the National Task Force on Student Aid Problems.

III.F. Data Processing in Student Aid

As aid programs have grown in size and complexity, the need for automated data processing systems and management information systems has also grown. Virtually all state and federal programs use computers to process student data. A majority of campus-based programs are supported with computers. However, the use of computers to support management information systems is still limited to the larger state programs and universities.

The primary reason why the use of computers by financial aid programs is limited is the initial cost of implementing systems. Another reason for their underutilization is lack of knowledge of the ways in which they could be used to make aid administration more efficient and effective. In the early 1970s, a national survey of college-based aid offices revealed that over half the respondents had not heard of the use of computers in financial aid decision-making (Jepson, 1973).

This lack of knowledge may be both a cause and a consequence of the relatively few publications concerned with data processing. Only eight items were identified for inclusion in this section. Although the technology for extensive use of computers has existed for over a decade (Brown, Janes, and Overman, 1967; College Entrance Examination Board, 1968) and has been promoted, it is likely to be some years before the technology is fully applied.

Among the documents cited below, Wooten (1974) offers a discussion on the need for and advantages of automated data systems, Bellia (1973) describes how the management information system works at a small college, and Miller (1975) discusses the use of computers in aid disbursement and loan collection.

III.F.1. Bellia, A. J. Computerized student financial aid reporting: How it works at a small private college. *Journal of Student Financial Aid,* Vol. 3, March 1973, pp. 39–44.

Describes the financial aid management information system at Canisius College.

III. F. 2. Brown, R. M., Janes, S. S., and Overman, I. O. *Computer applications to financial aid processing.* Iowa City, Iowa: American College Testing Program, 1967.

A description of various models and applications of computers to financial aid management on college campuses.

III. F. 3. College Entrance Examination Board. *Financial aid information systems.* White Plains, N.Y.: IBM, 1968.

Describes a computer-based system for processing financial aid applications and managing data and files in campus-based aid programs.

III. F. 4. Jepsen, K. J. *Computer decision making in student financial aid administration.* Bloomington, Ind.: Indiana University, 1973. (Dissertation)

Reports on a survey of 2,118 postsecondary institutions to determine the extent to which computers are used for financial aid decision-making. Found that out of 1,274 respondents 22 were currently using computers to package aid awards, 189 were planning to do so, 391 have decided against it, and 672 had never heard of it.

III. F. 5. Jepsen, K. J. and Buchanan, T. M. Financial aid decisions made by computer. *College Management,* Vol. 8, October 1973, pp. 17-18.

The authors demonstrate that the use of computers in packaging awards to individual students saves time and money in financial decisions.

III. F. 6. Jepsen, K. J., Matejka, L. E., and Hulet, R. E. Do more with less: "Computer packaging"—one possibility. *National Association of Student Personnel Administrators Journal,* Vol. 10, October 1972, pp. 156-160.

Provides a brief report on a survey of the use of computers in financial aid, then offers some suggestions on how their use will make aid administration more efficient.

III. F. 7. Miller, L. K. Computer assisted financial aid disbursement and loan collection. *Journal of Student Financial Aid,* Vol. 5, November 1975, pp. 27-34.

Describes the use of computers at Washington State University to control and report funds requested by, offered to, and disbursed to students. The system writes checks and performs loan collection functions according to federal regulations.

III. F. 8. Wooton, R. J. Business management and data systems for financial aid offices. In *Money, marbles, or chalk: Student financial support in higher education.* Keene, R., Adams, F. C., and King, J. E. (Eds.) Carbondale, Ill.: Southern Illinois University Press, 1975.

Discusses the principles of business management and the use of data processing systems in campus-based aid offices.

III.G. Scholarships, Grants, and Education Benefits

This section describes items related to the administration and management of scholarship and grant programs and programs offering education benefits. Scholarships and grants include awards of money, tuition discounts, remissions of tuitions and fees, or similar considerations that require neither repayment nor service to be performed by the recipient. Education benefits are those awards that accrue to students as a right by virtue of some previous service, such as veterans benefits; by virtue of payments made by students or their families, such as social security benefits; or, as a matter of public policy independent of student status, as in the case of welfare benefits or vocational rehabilitation awards.

Scholarships have the oldest history in the United States. Traditionally, they have been awarded to students who have exhibited some special talent, such as academic potential, athletic promise, or artistic ability, without regard to financial need. More recently, the majority of scholarship programs consider financial need as well as talent in their awards processes.

Grants are distinguished from scholarships in that they are awarded solely on the basis of financial need without considering the recipient's special talents or skills. Both scholarships and grants are especially valuable to students because they do not require repayment or service; they simply require that the recipient meet the academic standards of his postsecondary institution.

The underlying philosophy of scholarship and grant programs is that needy and deserving students should receive help to attend postsecondary institutions. These types of awards, which are frequently called "gift aid," represent the donor's investment in the education of the recipient. It is believed that such investments are justified because the donor, and society at large, will benefit from an educated citizenry. The degree to which governments support scholarship and grant programs is, in part, a consequence of the belief that society as well as individuals benefit from investments in the postsecondary education of students and that both should share the burden of its costs.

Those who believe that individual students benefit more from their education than does society as a whole are less likely to support scholarship and grant programs. Those who believe the most talented students should receive the greatest incentives to attend postsecondary education (because society may be more likely to receive benefits from their education) are most likely to support scholarship programs rather than grant programs. Furthermore, those who believe the most talented should receive incentives to attend postsecondary education are more likely to support scholarship awards without regard to financial need. These contrasting viewpoints are explicit and implicit in many of the items listed below.

Perhaps one of the most important developments in the awarding of grants to students has been the establishment and implementation of the federal Basic Educational Opportunity Grants (BEOG) Program. Authorized by the Higher Education Amendments Act of 1972, the BEOG Program was implemented in 1973 and will soon distribute over $1.7 billion annually to over 2 million students. The BEOG Program is an entitlement program. Every student who attends an eligible institution on at least a half-time basis is "entitled" to a grant of $1,400, less the amount the student and/or family can contribute, and limited to one-half the costs of attendance at the eligible institution. The programs' awards are considered the foundation upon which all aid from other sources will be built (or packaged).

The BEOG Program is important for the volume of awards it makes. But it is also important because it implements the beliefs that the education of needy students is an important societal investment and that needy students are entitled to educational opportunities simply by virtue of their citizenship and desire to receive education. Although the program has been widely lauded and accepted, it has produced its own set of controversies. Some of these are related to its system for determining the family contribution (see Chapter III, Section B). Others are related to award schedules and amounts (U.S. Congress, House Committee on Education and Labor, 1975); to its basic philosophy (Hansen and Lampman, 1974); or to its delivery system (Jones, 1974). BEOG and other grant programs are discussed in reports of congressional hearings (U.S. Congress, House Committee on Education and Labor, 1974, 1976).

Friedman and Thompson (1971) present the results of a national study on another large federal program, the Supplemental Education Opportunity Grants (SEOG) Program.

Although most grant programs make awards on the basis of the recipient's financial need, some institutionally funded programs do not. Johnson (1974) provides a model for the administration of a non-need-based program by a college or university.

Some scholarship and grant programs are funded by corporations for their employees and employees' dependents. Two publications provide very useful information and guidelines on the development and administration of corporate scholarship and fellowship programs (Council for Financial Aid to Education, 1975, 1976).

Another advantage of scholarship or grant awards over work-study or employment awards is that the former are not usually considered taxable income. Hopkins (1975) reviews recent court decisions on tax regulations regarding scholarships and fellowships.

Although approximately 35 percent of all the financial aid resources available to students is derived from educational benefits, relatively little attention has been paid to their distribution or impact. Consideration of these resources in need analysis is discussed in several items in Section III. B, but there are only four references in this section concerned with the administration of education benefits. Two deal with campus administration of education benefits (Hirsch, et al., 1976; Zimny and Williams, 1975) and two with the problems of monitoring awards to veterans under the G.I. Bill (Arstein, 1976; Risener, 1976).

Education benefits, which represent a significant proportion of total aid resources, are distributed unevenly and frequently without regard to the recipient's financial need. Because this distribution directly affects the ways in which other aid resources must be distributed to meet all student needs, more empirical data should be developed on who receives them and what their role in student and institutional finance is.

For additional items concerning scholarships, grants, and education benefits, see Chapter VII, Section B.

III. G. 1. Arstein, G. *The unbalanced two-step: Standards of progress for the* G.I. *Bill.* Washington, D.C.: National Advisory Council on Education Professions Development, 1976.

Discusses administrative problems of the G.I. Bill at institutional and national levels.

III. G. 2. Council for Financial Aid to Education. *Guidelines for a corporate fellowship program.* New York: Council for Financial Aid to Education, 1976.

Provides guidelines for establishing scholarship programs to support educated manpower for corporate success in a technological society. Degree and non-degree, undergraduate and graduate programs are discussed.

III. G. 3. Council for Financial Aid to Education. *How to develop and administer a corporate scholarship program.* New York: Council for Financial Aid to Education, 1975.

Survey responses from 17 companies and 15 company foundations on how to plan, administer, publicize, and review a corporate scholarship program.

III. G. 4. Friedman, N. and Thompson, J. The federal Educational Opportunity Grant Program. *Financial Aid Report,* Vol. 1, No. 2, December 1971.

Brief summary of the recommendations and findings of a national study of this federal program. Recommendations concern state allocation formulas, forward funding of the program, elimination of the distinction between initial and renewal monies, and establishment of regional advisory boards to help institutions set up programs.

III.G.5. Hansen, W. L. and Lampman, R. J. *Basic opportunity grants for higher education: Will the outcome differ from the intent?* Madison, Wis.: Institute for Research on Poverty, Wisconsin University, 1974.

The formula of the BEOG Program is tested against the theory and practice of negative income taxation. The key concept in both is that the family is the income-producing unit whose income must be counted in calculating benefits. Since many college students can't be held in dependent status as a part of a family unit, some of the arguments for the BEOG are considered questionable.

III.G.6. Hill, F. The Maryland scholarship scandal. *Change*, Vol. 4, June 1972, pp. 19–21.

Criticizes Maryland's scholarship program which makes awards on the basis of state senators' recommendations.

III.G.7. Hirsch, J. L., et al. Veteran and social security certification. *College and University*, Vol. 51, Summer 1976, pp. 777–780.

Report on a panel discussion on these topics.

III.G.8. Hopkins, B. R. Scholarships and fellowship grants: Current tax developments and problems. *Journal of College and University Law*, No. 3, Fall 1975, pp. 54–71.

Reviews recent rulings on what constitutes an excludable scholarship or fellowship grant for federal income tax purposes.

III.G.9. Johnson, B. G. *A model of the administration of an endowable non-financial need based scholarship program.* College Station, Tex: Texas A&M University, 1974 (Dissertation)

Documents the administration of the Texas A&M University Presidents' Scholars Award Program as a model for other nonfinancial need based programs.

III.G.10. Jones, R. N. Making the basic grant program more effective. *Journal of Student Financial Aid*, Vol. 4, November 1974, pp. 20–24.

Report of experience of students at Broome Community College, New York in getting information on and applying to the BEOG Program. Suggests changes in the BEOG delivery system to make it more effective.

III.G.11. Risener, R. The G.I. bilk. *Change*, Vol. 8, November 1976, pp. 20–21.

Discussion of the problems of G.I. Bill overpayments to Vietnam-era veterans.

III.G.12. U.S. Congress, House Committee on Education and Labor. *Basic Educational Opportunity Grant Program. Hearing before the Subcommittee on Postsecondary Education.* Washington, D.C.: Government Printing Office, 1975.

Hearings on proposed amendments to the BEOG family contribution schedule. Discussion of the Office of Education proposal to make adjustments in the assets reserves for families deriving income from salaries and wages and those of families deriving income from businesses and farms.

III.G.13. U.S. Congress, House Committee on Education and Labor. *Basic Educational Opportunity Grant Program: Hearings.* Washington, D.C.: Government Printing Office, 1976.

Hearings on proposed revisions to the BEOG Program. Presents testimony from representatives of public and private agencies.

III.G.14. U.S. Congress, House Committee on Education and Labor. *Student financial aid, Parts 4–6, graduate programs, state programs, grants.* Washington, D.C.: Government Printing Office, 1974.

Testimony from representatives of public and private agencies on aid to graduate students, state student aid programs, and various grant programs.

III.G.15. U.S. Office of Education. *Postsecondary institutions eligible for the basic grants program.* Washington, D.C.: Department of Health, Education, and Welfare, 1974.

Lists all postsecondary institutions whose students may be eligible to receive federal BEOG awards.

III.G.16. Winkler, K. J. State aid to students reaches $500 million a year. *Compact,* Vol. 9, December 1975, pp. 13–16.

Analyzes current data that indicates state scholarships are helping more and more students.

III.G.17. Zimny, J. D. and Williams, L. B., Jr. Veterans' and special programs. In *Money, marbles, or chalk: Student financial support in higher education.* Keene, R., Adams, F. C., and King, J. E. (Eds.) Carbondale, Ill.: Southern Illinois University Press. 1975.

Discusses the role of veterans' and special programs in providing student services and aid. Describes how these programs interface with aid office programs on college campuses.

III.H. Loans

Loans are awards of money made with the prior requirement that they subsequently be repaid in cash or service, in whole or in part, with or without interest.

To most policy-makers, loans are the most attractive form of student aid. This is because they must be repaid and, therefore, do not represent a direct expenditure but an investment of funds. Because they represent an investment and frequently collect interest, private as well as public capital can be effectively encouraged to support loan programs. Loans can be used to implement the philosophy that persons who derive benefits from education (the student consumers) should pay for its costs, without denying low-income students access to postsecondary education due to lack of current resources.

Loan programs are not without their disadvantages. Since the loans must be collected over generally long periods of time, loan programs cost more than other programs to administer. Recent experience with massive federal and state loan programs have shown that collection of loans is a frequently difficult, costly, and sometimes unsuccessful activity. Philosophically, the extensive or exclusive use of loan programs in student financial aid runs contrary to the belief that the public also benefits from an educated citizenry and, therefore, should support students through grants and/or institutional subsidies to keep costs to individuals at a minimum.

Furthermore, it is believed that low-income students, for whom equal opportunity is a major concern, are reluctant to accept large, long-term loans. Consequently, loan programs are potentially less effective than other types of aid programs in enhancing access, choice, and retention. Finally, because all educational and training programs do not produce equal monetary benefits, the extensive or exclusive use of loan programs to finance student costs ultimately discriminates against students whose programs lead to lower-income careers. This is because they have received a lower rate of return on their investment in a college education.

These issues have generated lengthy discussion and heated controversy which is evidenced in the literature of financial aid. Much of the controversy relates to federal loan programs, the largest in the nation. An overview of the early history of federal student loan programs is contained in a College Board study report (Kirkpatrick, 1968). Briefer, more recent explications of the issues regarding loans are offered by Hanford and Nelson (1970) and Hartman (1970). These two articles are especially interesting for their contrasting views. Hartman (1973) presents a more recent discussion of the future of student loan programs.

Contrasting opinions on this subject are found in five additional references (Alloway and Cordasco, 1976; Kaufman, 1972; Moore, 1975; U.S. Congress, House Committee on Education and Labor, 1974b; U.S. Congress, Senate Committee on Appropriations, 1976).

Two extensive studies of the federal Guaranteed Student Loan Program (GSLP) are concerned with most of the major administrative and philosophical issues of all loan programs (Systems Group, Inc., 1974; U.S. General Accounting Office, 1973).

One of the most controversial issues in loan programs is the default rate on repayments. Four items describe this problem, why it exists, and its implications for the future operation of loan programs (Mathis, 1973; U.S. Congress, House Committee on Education and Labor, 1974a; U.S. Congress, Senate Committee on Labor and Public Welfare, 1975; U.S. Congress, Senate Committee on Governmental Operations, 1976). Four articles contain specific suggestions and recommendations for improving loan collection processes and systems (Black, 1977; Maynard, 1974; Swift, 1976; Wolfe, 1974).

Several observers have advocated special kinds of loan programs to help alleviate the disadvantages of current ones. These are called income-contingent loan programs, They would make long-term loans to students whose repayment schedule would be determined on the amounts of income the students earned after completion of their education. It is believed that such programs would make loans more attractive to students, and consequently more effective; that repayments would be easier and more equitable, thereby reducing default rates; and that they would permit students to make greater contributions to the educational costs as payments for them would be spread out over a 20- or 25-year period.

Three early discussions and presentations of income-contingent loan programs are provided by Shapiro (1963a, 1963b) and Carlsson (1970). Probably the most comprehensive discussion of the issues, advantages, and disadvantages of income-contingent loan programs is provided by a report on a series of studies supported by the Ford Foundation (Johnstone, 1972a). Johnstone (1972b) and Kaufman (1973) list several fundamental questions which they believe must be answered before income-contingent loan policies can be developed. Wharton (1971) describes what are believed to be the dangers of such loan programs, that is, reduction of public support of higher education and increased inequities in its financing.

Five publications describe the operation of income-contingent loan programs at two institutions, Harvard University (Cooper, 1971; Gibson, 1972) and Yale University (Curran, 1973; The Yale Tuition Postponement Seminar, 1972; West, 1976).

Johnstone and Dresch (1972) describe how an income-contingent loan program could be incorporated into the federal Guaranteed Student Loan Program and Lawson, Johnson, and Lundun (1971) present a model for use by small colleges. Holdberg (1973) discusses the use of economic models to forecast the financial outcome of various repayment plans.

Further items on loans will be found in Chapter VII, Section VII.C.

III.H.1. Aiken, L. R., Jr. and Woodside, D. M. Some formulas and a computer program for determining payment schedules on student loans. *Journal of College Student Personnel,* Vol. 15, September 1974, p. 413.

Describes two formulas in use at Guilford College, North Carolina, for computing total periodic payments on student loans.

III.H.2. Alloway, D. N. and Cordasco, F. Student loans and higher education: A way out. *Intellect,* Vol. 104, January 1976, pp. 301–302.

Describes the establishment of a College Student Acceptance Corporation, which is needed to lend money to college students who don't qualify for free tuition programs.

III. H. 3. American Council on Education. New concepts of student access. *Policy Analysis Service Reports,* Vol. 1, No. 3, 1975.

Reports on a seminar on student aid programs, particularly issues concerning the National Direct Student Loan (NDSL) program.

III. H. 4. Berdon, R. I. Connecticut's "Susie Mae" program. *Financial Aid Report,* Vol. 2, November 1972.

Describes the purpose and operation of the state's model program to create a secondary market for student loans for postsecondary education.

III. H. 5. Black, R. W. Other students need money: An approach to the administration of revolving loan funds. *Journal of Student Financial Aid,* Vol. 7, May 1977, pp. 26–30.

Believes that campus financial aid administrators are not exercising the needed degree of responsibility in collecting loan funds to support new borrowers. Describes collection practices at a single university.

III. H. 6. Bowman, J. L. and Johnstone, D. B. Loans to parents: New help for the middle-income family. *College Board Review,* No. 98, Winter 1975–1976, pp. 24–30.

Describes the need for a national parental loan program that will lend amounts up to the total expected contribution less that portion which can reasonably be expected out of current purchasing power.

III. H. 7. Carlsson, R. J. A federal program of student loans. *American Journal of Economics and Sociology,* Vol. 24, July 1970, pp. 263–275.

The author discusses three proposals for federal income-contingent loan programs, describes their strength and weaknesses, and then offers a plan of his own.

III. H. 8. Cooper, W. K. SELF lets Harvard students financially help themselves: Student educational loan funds. *College and University Business,* Vol. 50, May 1971, pp. 54–56.

Describes Harvard University's Student Educational Loan Fund.

III. H. 9. Curran, W. E. Yale's tuition postponement option. *Journal of Law and Education,* Vol. 2, April 1973, pp. 283–288.

Discusses the Yale University plan, which bases student repayments of tuition loans on future earnings.

III. H. 10. Gibson, R. J. The new Harvard loan program. *Financial Aid Report,* Vol. 1, May 1972.

Describes the background and basis for establishment of the Harvard University income-contingent loan plan.

III. H. 11. Hanford, G. H. and Nelson, J. E. Federal student loan plans: The dangers are real. *College Board Review,* No. 75, Spring 1970, pp. 16–21.

Examines various plans for federal student loan programs. Concludes that there are too many unanswered questions about their impact on students and too little data available to answer the questions for policymakers to accept one or more proposals.

III. H. 12. Hartman, R. W. What next for student loans? *Financial Aid Report,* Vol. 2, March 1973.

Believes that the need determination requirement of the federal Guaranteed Student Loan Program (GSLP) limits consumer choice and that providing interest subsidies is bad federal policy. Proposes that consumers pay the costs of using loan monies for education and be provided with control over the decision to borrow money.

III. H. 13. Hartman, R. W. What's wrong with federal student loans? *College Board Review,* No. 77, Fall 1970, pp. 22-23.

Rejoinder to Hanford and Nelson's article on the dangers of federal student loan plans. Believes the provision of grants to low-income students and expansion of loans to all students is appropriate policy.

III. H. 14. Holdberg, R. D. *The Dresch-Goldberg VTL simulator model.* 1973. (ERIC — ED 093246, HE 005699)

Implementation of income-contingent loans requires either practical experience or the ability to predict the financial outcome of programs via models. Discussion of structure and computer implementation of one such model is offered.

III. H. 15. Ihlanfeldt, W. The university as lender. *Change,* Vol. 7, May 1975, pp. 46-47.

Discusses the problems of Northwestern University's participation in the Federally Insured Student Loan Program.

III. H. 16. Johnstone, D. B. *New patterns for college lending: Income contingent loans.* New York: Columbia University Press, 1972a,

Report on the Ford Foundation's studies on income contingent loans for higher education. Examines the current and projected pattern of educational finance, concluding that more manageable forms of loans will be needed to help students meet the costs. Analyzes different forms of programs and processes which colleges or student loan programs might use to suit their goals and resources. Also makes some recommendation for hybrid, fixed-schedule income-contingent loans within the federal Guaranteed Student Loan Program (GSLP).

III. H. 17. Johnstone, D. B. The role of income-contingent loans in financing higher education. *Educational Record,* Vol. 53, Spring 1972b, pp. 161-168.

Discusses several potential roles of income-contingent loans. Believes that the amount and form of lending must depend on the resolution of fundamental policies regarding the cost of higher education and the portions of these costs which should be passed on to students, parents, or taxpayers.

III. H. 18. Johnstone, D. B. and Dresch, S. P. *More manageable student loans: An institutional loan plan within the framework of the federal Guaranteed Student Loan Program.* New York: Ford Foundation, 1972.

Discusses the advantages of a hybrid income-contingent loan program which could operate within the current framework of the federal GSLP.

III. H. 19. Kaufman, H. Considering income-contingent loans. *Financial Aid Report,* Vol. 2, March 1973.

Poses a series of questions that should be answered by institutions before they develop an income-contingent loan program for students.

III. H. 20. Kaufman, H. Reform for loan plans? *Financial Aid Report,* Vol. 1, May 1972.

Calls for increased coordination among management and operation of federal student loan programs.

III. H. 21. Kirkpatrick, J. I. *A study of federal student loan programs.* New York: College Entrance Examination Board, 1968.

Analyzes the impacts, operations, and problems of six federally assisted loan programs: the National Direct Student Loan Program (NDSL), the Guaranteed Student Loan Program (GSLP), guaranteed loans for vocational students, the health professions student loan program, the nursing student loan program, and the Cuban refugee student loan program.

III. H. 22. Lawson, G., Johnson, M., and Lundun, D. *Income contingent loans: Conceptual and applied framework for the small college.* Bloomington, Ind.: Midwest Association of Student Financial Aid Administrators, 1971.

Presents a conceptual model and applied framework through which small colleges can implement income-contingent loan programs.

III. H. 23. Mathis, J. H. Defaults: Lowering cloud over the Guaranteed Loan Program. *Journal of Student Financial Aid,* Vol. 3, March 1973, pp. 27–31.

Discusses the economic, political, social and moral problems generated by increasing default rates.

III. H. 24. Mayes, C. R. Revamp the guaranteed loan program — And unlock the bank vault. *Journal of Student Financial Aid,* Vol. 3, November 1973, pp. 10–19.

Proposes the following changes in the federal GSLP: remove interest subsidies, allow lenders to discount the interest on loans, establish a central clearinghouse for records on borrowers, increase special allowance to lenders, and contract for "last resort" loans.

III. H. 25. Maynard, A. P. Suggestions for improving student loan billing procedures and collection techniques. *Journal of Student Financial Aid,* Vol. 4, June 1974, pp. 15–22.

Offers suggestions in three areas of loan administration: accounting and recordkeeping, collections, and reports. Comments on the need for changes in federal loan program regulations.

III. H. 26. Moore, D. R. The effects of changes in the Guaranteed Loan Program. *Journal of Student Financial Aid*, Vol. 5, May 1975, pp. 25–29.

States that change in the GSLP from making loans of convenience to loans of need has caused fewer students to borrow larger amounts of money at State University of New York College at Cortland.

III. H. 27. O'Leary, J. J. Financial community as a source of student loans funds. *Liberal Education*, Vol. 60, March 1974 (Supplement), pp. 94–99.

Discussion of the Student Loan Marketing Association and the commercial lending institutions as sources of student loans for college.

III. H. 28. Seals, J. D. Collection of university loans: A new alternative. *College Board Review*, No. 95, Spring 1975, pp. 6–12.

Discusses the effect large loans may have on a student's choice of college or vocation. Describes how income-contingent loans may alter these effects.

III. H. 29. Shapiro, E. Long-term student loans. *Harvard Educational Review*, Vol. 33, Spring 1963a, pp. 186–207.

One of the earlier proposals for a national income-contingent loan program to finance higher education. Discusses student eligibility, loan repayment schedules, and governmental costs.

III. H. 30. Shapiro, E. Long-term student loans, A reply. *Harvard Educational Review*, Vol. 33, Summer 1963b, pp. 360–378.

Responds to the critical review of the proposed income-contingent loan program by E. Green, J. F. Morse, and T. W. Schultz.

III. H. 31. Spencer, L. E. Risk measurement for short term loans. *Journal of Student Financial Aid*, Vol. 4, November 1974, pp. 30–35.

Presents a formula to help determine risks in student loan programs at colleges.

III. H. 32. Swift, J. Collecting national defense/direct student loans: Is it a financial aid office responsibility? *Journal of Student Financial Aid*, Vol. 6, February 1976, pp. 28–32.

Describes the financial aid office at the Cleveland Institute of Art and the institutional efforts to collect loans.

III. H. 33. Systems Group, Inc. GSLP *loan estimation model, Vol. 1–4*. Washington, D.C.: Systems Group, Inc., 1974.

Presents the history of the GSLP and an analysis of the data base used in the GSLP estimation model. The model can be used to predict student participation in the program by age, sex, race, gross and adjusted family income, and type of institution attended.

III. H. 34. U.S. Congress, House Committee on Education and Labor. *Guaranteed student loan amendments of 1976*. Washington, D.C.: Government Printing Office, 1976.

Hearings and testimony on the amendments to the federal Guaranteed Student Loan Program.

III.H.35. U.S. Congress, House Committee on Education and Labor. *Higher education loan programs. Hearings before the special Subcommittee on Education and Labor.* Washington, D.C.: Government Printing Office, 1974a.

Statements by public and private parties concerning interest and default rates in the GSLP.

III.H.36. U.S. Congress, House Committee on Education and Labor. *Student financial aid, Part 3, Student loan programs.* Washington, D.C.: Government Printing Office, 1974b.

Hearings and testimony on federal student loan programs.

III.H.37. U.S. Congress, Senate Committee on Appropriations. *Student loan programs. Senate hearing before the Committee on Appropriations. Fiscal year 1976.* Washington, D.C.: Government Printing Office, 1976.

Discusses loans to middle-income families, default rates, consumer protection, and views of lenders, aid administrators, and the Department of Health, Education, and Welfare.

III.H.38. U.S. Congress, Senate Committee on Labor and Public Welfare. *Examination into the high default rate and the new policy of the Department of Health, Education, and Welfare in regard to refunds due to students attending schools and how those refunds affect the amount of federal guarantee. Hearing before the Subcommittee on Education of the Committee on Labor and Public Welfare.* Washington, D.C.: Government Printing Office, 1975.

Discussions of the administration's attempts to deal with high default rates and HEW's policy on refunds due to students attending schools and how these affect the amount of federal guarantee.

III.H.39. U.S. Congress, Senate Committee on Government Operations, Permanent Subcommittee on Investigations. *Guaranteed student loan program: Hearings, Part 1 and Part 2.* Washington, D.C.: Government Printing Office, 1976.

Collection of testimony and exhibits on the federal GSLP program during November and December, 1975. Most testimonies were made by public officials.

III.H.40. U.S. General Accounting Office. *Improvements needed in administration of the Guaranteed Student Loan Program.* Washington, D.C.: Government Printing Office, 1973.

Describes administrative problems such as early notification of lenders when students leave college, ineffective collection efforts, defaults on student loans, and errors in billings. Makes recommendations for solutions.

III.H.41. West, E. G. The Yale tuition postponement plan in the mid-seventies. *Higher Education,* Vol. 5, May 1976, p. 169.

Discusses the income-contingent, loan-based tuition plan at Yale University and its experiences with interest rate crises and default rates.

III.H.42. Wharton, C. R. Dangers of income contingency loans. *College Management,* Vol. 6, December 1971, pp. 2–3.

Believes that widespread use of income-contingent loan plans would drastically reduce public support of higher education and increase inequities in financing students and institutions.

III.H.43. Whyte, H. E. The year of FISL. *Journal of Student Financial Aid*, Vol. 3, June 1973, pp. 12–18.

Reports on a survey of the Federally Insured Student Loan (FISL) policies of lending institutions in the San Diego, California area. Offers ten suggestions for counseling students on the FISL program.

III.H.44. Wolfe, H. G. How to collect delinquent accounts. *College Management*, Vol. 9, October 1974, pp. 11–12.

Describes the loan collections department established at Arizona State University.

III.H.45. Yale Tuition Postponement Seminar. *Proceedings*. New Haven, Conn.: Yale University, 1972.

Proceedings of a seminar on Yale University's tuition postponement plan. The plan links student educational costs to their ability to pay for that education over a working career through a type of income-contingent loan program.

III.I. Employment and Work-Study Programs

There are two kinds of employment of concern to aid administrators. The first is work-study employment which requires students to perform some service for a specific time in exchange for a specific sum of money. The second is term-time or summer employment that is not part of a financial aid package. The latter is important because self-help contributions to college costs are expected from these sources when financial need is determined.

Overviews of work-study program problems and issues are found in three lengthy publications (Adams and Stephens, 1970; Rauh, 1971; and U.S. Congress, House Committee on Education and Labor, 1974). Moore (1976) discusses a variety of effective programs in the United States and in foreign countries. Yaegel (1975) and Hay (1970) each assert that emphasis on student employment that is related to students' academic or career interests contributes to more effective work-study programs.

Friedman, Sanders, and Thompson (1974) briefly summarize the results of a national study of the federal College Work-Study Program (CWSP), the nation's largest. (See Section VII.D for another citation on this study.)

Most of the items cited in this section provide advice on establishing and operating employment and/or work-study programs. Work-study program employers include on-campus departments and divisions of institutions and off-campus agencies. Bates (1973) and Griffen and Lenz (1975) offer suggestions for the administration of on-campus programs; Burson (1975) and Edelstein (1975) discuss off-campus programs. Bolder (1975) asserts the importance of summer employment and describes a model program. Barnett (1973) examines the operation of a statewide summer employment program in North Carolina.

Adams and Stephens (1972) and Counts (1975) discuss job classification and pay policy plans for work-study employees. Citations of research on work-study and employment programs are offered in Section VII. D.

III.I.1. Adams, F. C. and Stephens, C. W. *A student job classification plan for colleges and universities.* Carbondale, Ill.: Southern Illinois University Press, 1972.

Describes a system which classifies student jobs and gives wage scales to help work-study employers determine salary rates and merit increases.

III.I.2. Adams, F. C. and Stephens, C. W. *College and university student work programs: Implications and implementations.* Carbondale, Ill.: Southern Illinois University Press, 1970.

Describes student employment philosophies, practices, and procedures and provides guidelines for operation of work-study programs.

III.I.3. Barnett, T. J., Jr. PACE—How summer employment opportunities were expanded in North Carolina. *Financial Aid Report,* Vol. 2, March 1973.

Describes a statewide summer work-study program established through the coordinated efforts of aid administrators, guidance counselors, and volunteers.

III.I.4. Bates, G. A. The utilization of on-campus employment in a student aid program. *Journal of Student Financial Aid,* Vol. 3, March 1973, pp. 32–38.

Describes the policies, practices, and operation of Stanford University's on-campus work-study program.

III.I.5. Bolder, D. A. Summer and vacation employment for college students. In *Money, marbles, or chalk: Student financial support in higher education.* Keene, R., Adams, F. C., and King, J. E. (Eds.) Carbondale, Ill.: Southern Illinois University Press, 1975.

Discusses the benefits of summer employment programs to students, institutions, and employers. Describes some components of a model program.

III.I.6. Burson, R. F. Student employment and the off-campus employer. In *Money, marbles, or chalk: Student financial support in higher education.* Keene, R., Adams, F. C., and King, J. E. (Eds.) Carbondale, Ill.: Southern Illinois University Press, 1975.

Discusses the advantages of off-campus work-study programs and offers some suggestions for implementing successful ones.

III.I.7. Cottam, K. M. Student employers in academic libraries. *College Research Libraries,* Vol. 31, July 1970, pp. 246–268.

Explores ways of minimizing dissatisfaction among library student assistants and maximizing their contributions to library work.

III.I.8. Counts, P. Pay policies for student workers. *Journal of Student Financial Aid*, Vol. 5, May 1975, pp. 5-11.

Reports on a survey of wage-payment policies at colleges in nine southern states. Study revealed that 37 percent of the colleges pay the minimum wage to all student workers and 63 percent pay differential rates.

III.I.9. Edelstein, F. *A guide to operating an off-campus college work-study program.* Washington, D.C.: National Association of Student Financial Aid, 1975.

Provides information, ideas, and suggestions to help institutional aid administrators develop or expand off-campus work-study programs. The guide includes models and sample materials.

III.I.10. Friedman, N., Sanders, L., and Thompson, J. The federal College Work-Study Program. *Financial Aid Report*, Vol. 3, January 1974.

Brief report on the conclusions and recommendations of a national study on the federal College Work-Study Program. Recommendations concern use of trained placement counselors, increasing off-campus employer contribution to student earnings, extending participation to profit-making organizations, and granting academic credit for CWSP experience.

III.I.11. Griffen, J. R. and Lenz, C. D. The on-campus student work program. In *Money, marbles, or chalk: Student financial support in higher education.* Keene, R., Adams, F. C., and King, J. E. (Eds.) Carbondale, Ill.: Southern Illinois University Press, 1975.

Offers suggestions on the implementation and organization of campus work-study programs.

III.I.12. Hay, J. E., et al. Student part time jobs: Relevant or nonrelevant. *Vocational Guidance Quarterly*, Vol. 19, December 1970, pp. 113-118.

Study found that students with jobs relevant to their major achieve better grades than those with nonrelevant jobs, that students working more than 15 hours per week earn lower grade-point averages than those working fewer hours, and that students working a moderate number of hours do as well as or better than nonworking students.

III.I.13. Moore, R. S. Work-study: Education's sleeper? *Phi Delta Kappan*, Vol. 57, January 1976, pp. 322-327.

Discusses effective work-study programs in the United States and in foreign countries.

III.I.14. Rauh, M. A. *The advantages of work-study plans.* New York: Academy for Educational Development, 1971.

Describes the practices and policies of several work-study program models.

III.I.15. Russo, J. A. Off-campus college work-study: An alternative approach. *Journal of Student Financial Aid*, Vol. 2, May 1972, pp. 13-18.

Discusses recent revisions in federal CWSP regulations on off-campus student employment and their implementation at Le Moyne College, New York.

III.I.16. U.S. Congress, House Committee on Education and Labor. *Student financial assistance (work programs); Hearings before the Special Subcommittee on Education and Labor.* Washington, D.C.: Government Printing Office, 1974.

Reports on six days of testimony on the College Work-Study Program. Data on positive and negative aspects of the program are presented.

III.I.17. Weiss, K., et al. The work-study approach at undergraduate and graduate levels. *Journal of Chemical Education,* Vol. 50, June 1973, pp. 408–411.

Discusses the philosophy and practice of an experimental cooperative education project.

III.I.18. Yaegel, J. S. The "study" part of a work-study program. *Journal of Business Education,* Vol. 50, January 1975, pp. 151–153.

The author believes that emphasis on the study part of work-study programs may provide the opportunity to achieve the program's real objectives.

III.J. Programs for Special Student Groups

The administration of all aid programs requires adherence to the same basic principles and practices. However, some special considerations arise when the programs serve particular subgroups of students. The items listed here are concerned with such considerations and subgroups.

Students from minority/poverty backgrounds represent one special group. It is generally believed that these students need more personal counseling from aid administrators, particularly on available aid resources and budgeting for college costs. It is also argued that minority/poverty students may need additional financial support to pay for items routinely available to more affluent students. One of the most important needs of minority students is the opportunity to communicate freely and openly with financial aid administrators who are sensitive to student ethnicity, as well as student financial needs (Baker, 1971; Clair, 1975; Fordyce, 1973; Green, 1975; McClellan, 1970; Parker, 1974; Penn and Vejil, 1976; Shepherd, 1975).

Two of the following publications discuss programs especially designed for minority students—one a grant program supported by faculty contributions (Arden, 1970) and the second a work-study program operating in a major metropolitan area (East-West Gateway Coordinating Council, 1973).

Independent students form another group presenting special problems for aid administrators. The first problem is determining who should be considered independent of parental support for financial aid purposes. Although there are program criteria for establishing the financial aid eligibility of an independent student, there is some question as to whether these criteria are legal (Barkin, 1975; Fife, 1976).

Even if the current criteria are legal, there are those who question their equity and justness. A collection of papers from a College Board conference contains discussions of legal, financial, social, and psychological implications of providing aid to these students (College Entrance Examination Board, 1974).

Van Dusen (1975) describes several alternative definitions of independent students and their implications for the distribution of student aid among all groups of students. Barton (1976) and Burnett (1972) analyze the definitions and policies regarding independent students at midwestern colleges and universities.

The administration of financial aid programs for professional school students is the topic of three articles (Crippan et al., 1976; Tragesser, et al., 1970; Weiler, 1976). Other items concern aid to foreign students (Dakak, 1975), aid to veterans (Repp, 1977; U.S. Congress, House Committee on Veterans' Affairs, 1974), aid to students incarcerated in prison systems (Catillaz and Russo, 1976), and aid to dependents of college faculty members (Huntly, 1970; Wilbanks, 1972).

Married students, transfer students, and part-time students also present problems for financial aid administrators. Surprisingly, only one reference for each of these groups is listed below. It is surprising because over 830,000 students in postsecondary education are married; at least a million students transfer between schools each year; and nearly 4.4 million students are enrolled on a part-time basis.

One special problem with the administration of aid to married students concerns determination of their student expense budgets. Sauber (1971) discusses this issue and the experiences at eight colleges. Another problem, involving the determination of the married student's ability to pay for educational and maintenance expenses, is discussed by some items in Section III.B. But very little empirical data are found in the literature on the ways in which married students' educational costs, family resources, and financial aid resources affect their access, choice, and retention. Because married students represent a special subgroup for treatment in need analysis, and because they represent a substantial number of all students, much more should be known about their patterns of educational financing.

A primary concern in providing aid to transfer students relates to whether the needy transfer student receives aid in amounts and types equivalent to those provided to the needy freshman student (Brienza, 1973). Because more and more students transfer between colleges, especially from community colleges to four-year institutions, more data should be gathered on the extent to which their financial needs are met. The amounts of aid available to students who transfer from community colleges to four-year colleges are especially significant in postsecondary educational systems that view community colleges as the point of entry for students from low-income families. Without access to aid at four-year colleges, financially needy students may have to discontinue their educations at the end of two years.

Almost four out of every ten students enrolled in postsecondary education are enrolled on a part-time basis. In recent years, part-time student enrollment has increased at a much more rapid rate than full-time student enrollment. The financial aid needs of part-time students are real, significant, and frequently unmet (Committee on the Financing of Higher Education for Adult Students, 1974). Because part-time enrollments are increasing, partially in response to increasing costs of full-time attendance, more data on part-time student financing patterns should be collected and analyzed. Current data are insufficient to determine how financial aid programs can or should be modified to assist the part-time student.

Additional items on the administration of financial aid to special student groups are located in Chapter VII, Section VII. F.

III.J.1. Arden, E. King scholars at C. W. Post College. *Today's Education,* Vol. 59, September 1970, p. 72.

Describes a minority-student scholarship program supported by monetary contributions from the faculty.

III.J.2. Baker, W. The financial aid office and minority students. In *The minority student on the campus: Expectations and possibilities.* Altman, R. A. and Snyder, P. O. (Eds.) Boulder, Colo.: Western Interstate Commission for Higher Education, 1971.

Argues that financial aid administrators should maintain and emphasize their humanness in working with minority students and in representing the students' interests to faculty and staff.

III.J.3. Barkin, T. G. Legal implications of Office of Education criteria for the self-supporting student. *Journal of College and University Law,* Vol. 2, Spring 1975, pp. 229–247.

Discusses the Office of Education's regulations regarding need analysis for self-supporting students. Concludes that the guidelines are constitutional, but recommends new flexibility.

III.J.4. Barton, X., et al. Independent student policies and practices in Michigan. *Journal of Student Financial Aid,* Vol. 6, February 1976, pp. 3–10.

Summarizes a survey of institutional policies regarding financial aid to self-supporting students.

III.J.5. Brienza, R. J. Can we aid the transfer student? *Financial Aid Report,* Vol. 3, September 1973.

Contends that it is possible to treat freshmen and transfer students' financial needs in an equitable fashion if there is better articulation between two-year and four-year colleges *and* if state aid programs agree to permit two-year college graduates to apply for scholarships.

III.J.6. Burnett, D. D. *The administration of financial aid for financially independent students at big ten universities.* Bloomington, Ind.: Indiana University, 1972. (Dissertation)

Analyzes definitions used by aid administrators to identify independent students and examines the attitudes and perceptions of the administrators toward problems related to providing them with aid.

III.J.7. Catillaz, M. J. and Russo, J. A. The funding of prison education programs: An approach. *Journal of Student Financial Aid,* Vol. 6, November 1976, pp. 52–56.

Offers suggestions on the funding of educational programs for inmate-students.

III.J.8. Clair, J. Black perspective on higher education. *Journal of Student Financial Aid,* Vol. 5, March 1975, pp. 17–23.

Discussion of the need for black colleges and public support of their programs and students.

III.J.9. College Entrance Examination Board. *Who pays? Who benefits? A national invitational conference on the independent student.* New York: College Entrance Examination Board, 1974.

Collection of papers concerning independent students. Discusses legal, financial, social, and psychological implications of student independence for financial aid purposes.

III.J.10. Committee on the Financing of Higher Education for Adult Students. *Financing part-time students: The new majority in postsecondary education.* Washington, D.C.: American Council on Education, 1974.

Final report and recommendation of the committee. Describes characteristics of part-time students, trends in their enrollment, and ways in which their educational costs are met. Concludes that part-time students were discriminated against in federal, state, and institutional aid programs and in tuition charges. Discusses the patterns of financing adult students in other countries and recent proposals for their financing in the United States.

III.J.11. Comptroller General of the United States. *Coordination needed in the award of financial aid to Indian students. Report to the Senate Committee on Interior and Insular Affairs.* Washington, D.C.: Government Printing Office, 1975.

This report surveys the Office of Education, Bureau of Indian Affairs, state financial aid associations, and higher education institutions to determine policies and practices for developing financial aid packages for American Indian students.

III.J.12. Crippan, J. P. et al. Centralized admissions and financial aid services center for professional schools. *College and University,* Vol. 51, Summer 1976, pp. 503–508.

Report on a panel discussion of the advantages and disadvantages of centralized systems in use at various professional schools.

III.J.13. Dakak, F. Problems of foreign students. In *Money, marbles, or chalk: Student financial support in higher education.* Keene, R., Adams, F. C., and King, J. E. (Eds.) Carbondale, Ill.: Southern Illinois University Press, 1975.

Suggests ways by which financial aid administrators can and should help foreign students.

III.J.14. East-West Gateway Coordinating Council. *Minority work-study program.* St. Louis, Mo.: East-West Gateway Coordinating Council, 1973.

Describes a work-study program in St. Louis that provides employment and training for minority graduate and upper-division undergraduate students.

III.J.15. Fife, J. D. *The independent student and student aid problems.* Washington, D.C.: American Association for Higher Education, 1976.

Discusses the legality of restrictions on students over 18 declaring themselves financially independent of their parents. Examines assumptions regarding parental financial support and reviews regulations and court decisions on the topic.

III.J.16. Fordyce, H. R. Counselors in a talent search and encouragement program view college financial aid procedures. *Financial Aid Report,* Vol. 2, March 1973.

Discusses the financial aid process from the point of view of counselors in Project Opportunity. Offers suggestions for improvement of the process.

III.J.17. Fordyce, H. R. Financial independence among college students. *Financial Aid Report,* Vol. 3, September 1973.

Discusses HEW guidelines defining independent student status for financial aid purposes. Considers these guidelines in relation to new court decisions on the emancipation of 18-year-olds.

III.J.18. Green, R. L. Minority admissions and support. *Journal of Student Financial Aid,* Vol. 5, March 1975, pp. 24–31.

Observations on admissions practices and support services, including financial aid, for black and other minority students at predominantly white colleges and universities.

III.J.19. Huntly, C. W. Faculty children rate special tuition help from colleges. *College and University Business,* Vol. 49, August 1970, pp. 40–41.

Reports on a survey of problems and policies regarding tuition aid programs for faculty children at 30 northeastern colleges.

III.J.20. Klingelhofer, E. L. Do race and economics decide who gets what? *Journal of Student Financial Aid,* Vol. 1, May 1971, pp. 34–45.

Explains why race and economics do influence who receives financial aid.

III.J.21. Lennon, F., et al. *The beginning of a journey. A report on minority programs in predominantly white dental schools.* Cambridge, Mass.: Abt Associates, Inc., 1974.

Report on a workshop on minority education in dentistry. Discusses academic and financial barriers to dental school for minority students and the potential costs of alleviating these barriers.

III.J.22. Mason, H. R. Effectiveness of student aid programs tied to a service commitment. *Journal of Medical Education,* Vol. 46, July 1971, pp. 575-583.

Discusses scholarship and loan programs designed to encourage medical students to practice in rural areas.

III.J.23. McClellan, F. M. A black student looks at the present system of financial aid. *College Board Review,* No. 77, Fall 1970, pp. 10-12.

Describes black students' problems with the processes of application for admissions and financial aid. Believes employment of black administrators would help to alleviate these problems.

III.J.24. Montgomery, G., et al. *Federal agencies and black colleges. Fiscal years 1972 and 1973.* Washington, D.C.: Federal Interagency Committee on Education, 1976.

Reports on data from 23 federal departments regarding funds awarded to 114 predominantly black colleges. Compares this data to data for all higher education.

III.J.25. Nelson, B. W., et al. An analysis of the Educational Opportunity Bank for medical student financing. *Journal of Medical Education,* Vol. 47, August 1972, pp. 603-611.

Discusses the potential for public- and private-funded EOB programs for loans to medical students. Argues that only a federally supported bank will be attractive to students and private lenders.

III.J.26. Parker, S. A. *The effect of financial assistance and counseling on the educational practice of minority students in an urban public university.* Evanston, Ill.: Northwestern University, 1974. (Dissertation)

Presents research on the experiences of 100 freshmen at Chicago State University. Found that financial aid does not affect the rate of attrition but does contribute to higher student grade-point averages and a higher rate of graduation.

III.J.27. Penn, R. and Vejil, E. Financial aid for minority students: Improving the odds. *Journal of Student Financial Aid,* Vol. 6, May 1976, pp. 4-8.

Cites four critical factors in the process of delivering financial assistance to minority students: providing students, parents and counselors with information; keeping communication clear and concise; helping minority students learn to manage money; and maintaining periodic communication with aid applicants and recipients.

III.J.28. Repp, C. A. Monitoring veterans support. *Journal of Student Financial Aid,* Vol. 7, February 1977, pp. 45-49.

Provides suggestions for management of support programs for veterans on college campuses.

III.J.29. Rhine, E. E., et al. Admissions and financial aid for minority students at professional schools. *College and University*, Vol. 46, Summer 1971, pp. 426–430.

Report on a panel discussion offering recommendations for aid administrators and admissions officers.

III.J.30. Sauber, S. R. Money and marriage in college. *College and University*, Vol. 46, Spring 1971, pp. 245–250.

Compares married student budgets used by aid administrators at eight universities. Discusses the financial aid policies for married students at each institution.

III.J.31. Shepherd, R. E. Student support and the black student. In *Money, marbles, or chalk: Student financial support in higher education*. Keene, R., Adams, F. C., and King, J. E. (Eds.) Carbondale, Ill.: Southern Illinois University Press, 1975.

Believes that financial aid programs are adequate to remove financial barriers but that administrators should be more attentive to the removal of psychological or attitudinal barriers.

III.J.32. Tragesser, G., et al. Financial aid programs for professional schools. *College and University*, Vol. 45, Summer 1970, pp. 461–468.

Report on a panel discussion of student aid problems at professional schools.

III.J.33. U.S. Congress, House Committee on Veterans' Affairs. *Separate tuition payments for Vietnam era veterans. Hearings before the Subcommittee on Education and Training of the Committee on Veterans' Affairs*. Washington, D.C.: Government Printing Office, 1974.

Statements and testimony on separate tuition payments for Vietnam-era veterans.

III.J.34. U.S. Congress, Senate Committee on Labor and Public Welfare. *Health professions education assistance act of 1976*. Washington, D.C.: Government Printing Office, 1976.

Hearings and testimony on federal financial aid programs to aid students in the health professions.

III.J.35. Van Dusen, W. D. Alternative definitions of the self-supporting student. *Journal of Student Financial Aid*, Vol. 5, May 1975, pp. 30–33.

Alternative definitions of independent students are described and tested against present BEOG definitions to determine what changes would occur in the present distribution of dependent and independent students.

III.J.36. Weiler, W. C. Loans for medical students: The issue of manageability. *Journal of Medical Education*, Vol. 51, June 1976, pp. 447–453.

Analyzes the limitations of the federal GSLP in financing costs of education for medical students.

III.J.37. Wilbanks, J. J. Tuition remission and the faculty child. *AAUP Bulletin,* Vol. 58, December 1972, pp. 419–421.

Contends that tuition remissions should not be offered to children of faculty members, primarily because the practice is not in keeping with the concept of equal opportunity.

III.K. Aid Administration at Specific Types of Institutions

Because the basic principles, practices, and problems of all aid programs are similar, most of the literature on the administration of student aid programs is not concerned with problems at specific types of institutions. There are, however, a substantial number of publications concerned with aid administration at community and junior colleges.

Aid administration at these types of institutions is relatively recent. Community colleges, because of their low- or no-tuition policies have historically given little attention to student aid requirements, assuming that low tuitions alleviated most financial needs. In recent years, however, it has been discovered that community college students' financial aid needs are real and substantial.

Articles by Fordyce (1971) and Miller (1971) were among the earliest to discuss the need for expansion of financial aid programs at these institutions. A national study by the College Board on the impact of federal aid programs on community colleges drew a great deal of attention to student aid needs (Gladieux, 1975; Nelson, 1976).

Four dissertations on the administration of aid at community colleges in California, Illinois, Maryland, and Pennsylvania provide helpful data on financial aid programs and impacts in those states (Angove, 1973a; Bers, 1970; Johnson, 1973; Snyder, 1971). Three items examine the administration of aid at single community colleges (Angove, 1973b; Harris, 1973; Lewis, 1977).

Eckert and Murphy (1976) have provided a functional model for community college financial aid offices which is based, in part, on Eckert's (1973) earlier research. Russo (1976) examines the current problems of aid administration and offers some suggestions to alleviate them.

Only three items in this section deal with aid administration practices and problems at other types of institutions, namely, state universities (White and Schulke, 1973), state colleges (Pernal, 1973), and small colleges (Sidar, 1966).

In view of the recent growth in the body of financial aid literature on community colleges, it is likely that observations on the administration of aid at public and private business, trade, and vocational-technical schools may soon begin to appear. Aid programs are growing at these institutions, which are in a situation approximating that of community colleges a decade ago. There is a need for research on the aid policies, practices, and problems at these types of institutions.

III. K. 1. Angove, B. C. *A study of financial aids programs in California community colleges.* Los Angeles: University of Southern California, 1973a. (Dissertation)

Surveys financial aid programs, services, organizations, personnel, committees, relationships to other college campus offices, philosophies, and policies at 92 community colleges.

III. K. 2. Angove, G., et al. *Modesto Junior College, A study of the financial aid program.* Modesto, Calif.: Modesto Junior College, 1973b.

Analysis of the financial aid program at Modesto Junior College, and the characteristics, needs, resources, and plans of the students it serves.

III. K. 3. Bers, H. M. *An investigation into financial aids practices in Illinois public junior colleges.* Urbana, Ill.: University of Illinois, 1970. (Dissertation)

Investigates the financial aid offices, staffs, administrative structures, awarding methods and procedures, perceived strengths and weaknesses, and types of aid available to students at 39 colleges.

III. K. 4. Eckert, M. A. *Development of a functional model for a community-junior college financial aid office by the Delphi technique.* Commerce, Tex.: East Texas State University, 1973. (Dissertation)

Identifies the functions of a model aid office, then compares the functions of Texas community-junior college offices to the model. Describes 99 functions in 10 major categories.

III. K. 5. Eckert, M. A. and Murphy, H. D. A functional model for a community-junior college financial aid office. *Journal of Student Financial Aid,* Vol. 6, November 1976, pp. 5–12.

Report on a research project to identify the functions that should be performed by a model community-junior college financial aid office and the application of the model to evaluate aid offices at two-year colleges in Texas.

III. K. 6. Fordyce, J. W. Financial aid in the community college. *Financial Aid Report,* Vol. 1, September 1971.

Examines the current financial situation for community college students and questions whether current patterns of financial support reflect the purposes and objectives held by members of the financial aid community.

III. K. 7. Gladieux, L. E. Federal financial aid funds – Are the two-year colleges being short-changed? *College Board Review,* No. 96, Summer 1975, pp. 10–15.

Report on the distribution of federal student aid dollars to postsecondary institutions. The lack of aid available to community college students is attributed to institutional philosophy, financial structures, and the operation of their financial aid programs.

III.K.8. Harris, M. I. Student financial aid. *New Directions for Community Colleges,* Vol. 1, Summer 1973, pp. 65–75.
Detailed description of administration of student aid at one community college.

III.K.9. Johnson, B. M. *Financial aid programs, operations, resources, needs and projections in Maryland community colleges.* Washington, D.C.: Catholic University of America, 1973. (Dissertation)
Investigates the operation of aid programs on 14 campuses; reviews the policies and procedures governing them; and determines the amounts and types of resources available to students by family income levels, residence, and enrollment status.

III.K.10. Lewis, C. Alternatives in community college financial aid administration. *Journal of Student Financial Aid,* Vol. 7, February 1977, pp. 17–23.
Describes financial aid policies and practices at Fort Steilacoom Community College, Washington, especially as they relate to service to nontraditional students.

III.K.11. Miller, G. S. The community college: Upstart on the financial aid scene. *Journal of Student Financial Aid,* Vol. 1, November 1971, pp. 22–27.
Describes the availability and management of student aid resources at community colleges and criticizes the small aid programs, low commitment to student aid, poorly trained financial aid personnel, and poorly staffed offices. Makes suggestions for improvement.

III.K.12. Nelson, J. E. Student aid at the two-year college: Who gets the money? *Community and Junior College Journal,* Vol. 47, October 1976, p. 12.
Describes how misperceptions of student costs, unavailability of aid to part-time students, and lack of skilled staff at community colleges contribute to their underparticipation in federal student aid programs.

III.K.13. Pernal, M. State colleges and the middle income student: A dilemma for the financial aid officer. *College and University,* Vol. 48, Winter 1973, pp. 84–86.
Discusses the financial aid problems of middle-income students who want to enroll at state colleges. Suggests some administrative ways to help resolve the problems.

III.K.14. Russo, J. A. Community college student aid: A hard look from within. *Journal of Student Financial Aid,* Vol. 6, February 1976, pp. 20–27.
Discusses the problems of financial aid administration at community colleges and some attempts to alleviate them.

III.K.15. Sidar, A. G. Where small college financial aid programs go wrong. *College Board Review,* No. 61, Fall 1966, pp. 23–26.
Offers observations on institutional policies and practices which are inefficient and ineffective in student aid administration. Believes that small colleges are

most likely to err when their aid programs are aimed toward meeting institutional rather than student needs.

III. K. 16. Simmons, H. I. and Blocker, C. E. The reality of student finances. *New Directions for Community Colleges,* Vol. 2, Winter 1974, pp. 49–56.

The authors believe that community college students are discriminated against by aid policies designed to serve traditional rather than nontraditional students.

III. K. 17. Snyder, F. A. *Financial assistance in selected Pennsylvania community colleges and its relationship to persistence and achievement.* College Park, Md.: University of Maryland, 1971. (Dissertation)

Subjects included recipients and nonrecipients as full-time students in Fall, 1967. Found that the two groups did not differ in achievement and persistence when effects of high school rank and family income were held constant.

III. K. 18. U.S. Congress, House Committee on Education and Labor. *Student financial aid, Part 7, Institutional aid.* Washington, D.C.: Government Printing Office, 1974.

Hearings before the Subcommittee on Education include testimony from public and private agencies on institutional financial aid programs.

III. K. 19. White, M. R. and Schulke, B. K. Iowa State University's financial aid system. *Financial Aid Report,* Vol. 3, September 1973.

Describes the operation of the computer-assisted aid program at Iowa State University.

III.L. Financial Aid Program Annual Reports

The number of annual reports produced by financial aid programs has increased with the expansion of aid programs themselves and of public interest in them. Many of these reports are collected each year by the Educational Resources Information Center (ERIC) and are thus more readily available to interested readers.

These documents are helpful in understanding each program's history, goals, policies, practices, and the characteristics of aid recipients. They are particularly useful to researchers who are interested in assessment of the distribution of aid among various populations. Some of the more readily available items are listed here.

III. L. 1. Alabama Postsecondary 1202 Commission. *Alabama student assistance program, first annual report, 1975–76 academic year.* Montgomery, Ala.: Alabama Postsecondary 1202 Commission, 1976.

Statistical description of characteristics and county residences of recipients of state grants.

III.L.2. Boozer, H. R. *Annual report of the South Carolina Commission on Higher Education.* Columbia, S.C.: South Carolina Commission on Higher Education, 1976.

Reviews major activities and concerns of the commission. Statistical data are provided for several educational programs, including student aid.

III.L.3. Boyd, J. D. *National Association of State Scholarship Aid Grant Programs. 8th annual survey, 1976-77 academic year.* Deerfield, Ill.: National Association of State Scholarship Programs, 1976.

Report on the policies, practices, and awards of state and territorial comprehensive grant programs. Includes statistical data for 1975-76 and 1976-77. (Published annually)

III.L.4. California State Student Aid Commission. *Tenth biennial report, July, 1974-June 30, 1976.* Sacramento, Calif.: California State Student Aid Commission, 1976.

Describes the policy changes, achievement and problems of seven programs administered by the commission. Statistical data on program awards and recipients are included.

III.L.5. Commission of Higher Education. *Annual report to the board of regents of the Montana University System, 1973-74.* Helena, Mont.: Montana University System, 1974.

Contains comprehensive data on programs and policies of six institutions in the state university system. Includes statistical data on financing, enrollments, federal programs, and financial aid.

III.L.6. Council for Postsecondary Education. *Annual status report on expenditures in state need grant and state work-study programs.* Olympia, Wash.: Washington State Council for Postsecondary Education, 1976.

Reports on the distribution of state aid to students and institutions in Washington.

III.L.7. Danforth Foundation. *The Danforth and Kent fellowships: A quinquennial review.* St. Louis, Mo.: Danforth Foundation, 1976.

Reviews the objectives, philosophy, and procedures of the programs. Contains statistical data on personal, academic, and employment characteristics of fellowship winners.

III.L.8. Illinois State Scholarship Commission. *Report.* Deerfield, Ill.: Illinois State Scholarship Commission, 1975.

Reports on nine state-authorized and state-funded programs for Illinois postsecondary students. Includes statistical data on programs and recipients.

III.L.9. Iowa State Higher Education Facilities Commission. *1973-75 biennium report.* Des Moines, Iowa: Iowa State Higher Education Facilities Commission, 1975.

Reports on four federal and four state programs providing direct benefits to postsecondary education in the state. Statistics are provided for each program, including student aid programs.

III. L. 10. Lind, M. L. *Annual report for 1972-73 of the student financial aid programs.* Juneau, Alaska: Alaska State Department of Education, 1973.

A longitudinal review of growth and changes in the state's loan and grant programs, including statistical and survey information on programs and recipients.

III. L. 11. Maryland Higher Education Loan Corporation. *Annual report to the governor and the general assembly of Maryland.* Baltimore, Md.: Maryland Higher Education Loan Corporation, 1974.

Report on budgeting characteristics of the loan program and the characteristics of its lenders and borrowers.

III. L. 12. Michigan State Department of Education. *Annual report 1973-74: Michigan department of education student financial assistance services.* Lansing, Mich.: Michigan State Department of Education, 1974.

Covers four basic areas of services provided by the department: the guaranteed loan program, the competitive scholarship program, the tuition grant program, and the special education program.

III. L. 13. Ohio Board of Regents. *Ohio instructional grants, Fifth annual report, 1974-75 academic year.* Columbus, Ohio: Ohio Board of Regents, 1975.

Describes the grant program's policies and practices, and profiles the financial aspects and characteristics of students involved in the program.

III. L. 14. Pennsylvania Higher Education Assistance Agency. *Annual report for 1973-74.* Harrisburg, Pa.: Pennsylvania Higher Education Assistance Agency, 1974.

Covers the state higher education grant program, the state loan guaranty program, and the matching-funds program.

III. L. 15. Pennsylvania Higher Education Assistance Agency. *State higher education grant program. Comparative summary statistics, 1972-73 versus 1973-74.* Harrisburg, Pa.: Pennsylvania Higher Education Assistance Agency, 1974.

Reports on the number and characteristics of recipients of state higher education grant program awards.

III. L. 16. South Carolina Higher Education Tuition Grants Committee. *Annual report.* Columbia, S.C.: South Carolina Higher Education Tuition Grants Committee, 1975.

Covers the history, philosophy, statutory authority, and expenditures and resources for the program. Statistical appendix provides detailed description of characteristics of award recipients.

III. L. 17. State Education Commission. *The Kansas tuition grant program, 1972-73, A report of the first year.* Topeka, Kans.: State Education Commission, 1972.

Provides a detailed analysis of the background, implementation, and operation of the program. Describes the distribution of aid to students at different types of institutions, and emphasizes the program's effect on private institutions. Offers recommendations for strengthening the program.

III.L.18. State Education Assistance Authority. *Annual report.* Raleigh, N.C.: State Education Assistance Authority, 1976.

Reports on the distribution of state-supported aid program dollars to students and institutions in North Carolina.

III.L.19. State Scholarship Commission. *Academic Year 1974–1975, Annual report.* Hartford, Conn.: Connecticut State Scholarship Commission, 1975.

Tenth annual report on the state's aid programs. Includes statistical data on the scholarship program, restricted educational achievement program, college continuation grant program, higher education grant program, and state work-study program.

III.L.20. Tennessee Student Assistance Corporation. *Preliminary report on the activities of the TSAC for the school year 1974–75.* Nashville, Tenn.: Tennessee Student Assistance Corporation, 1975.

Describes the merger of the state loan corporation and student assistance agency. Reports on the administration of four state assistance programs.

III.L.21. Texas College and University System. *Texas higher education, 1968–1980. A report to the 64th Texas legislature.* Austin, Tex.: Coordinating Board, Texas College and University System, 1975.

Emphasizes structure, governance, enrollments, postsecondary opportunity, faculty and staff, facilities, financing higher education, and student costs and assistance.

III.L.22. Texas College and University System. *1975 annual report and statistical supplement to the annual report.* Austin, Tex.: Coordinating Board, Texas College and University System, 1975.

Report highlights and summarizes the work of the Coordinating Board. Statistical supplement presents data on enrollments, programs, faculty salaries, campus development and finance, and the state student loan program.

III.L.23. U.S. Office of Education. *Annual report of the U.S. Commission of Education.* Washington, D.C.: Government Printing Office, 1974.

Describes the activities of the Office of Education in 1973; discusses the condition of education from the viewpoint of finance, educational quality, and equal access.

III.L.24. Vermont Student Assistance Corporation. *Report to the Vermont general assembly for fiscal years ended 1973 and 1974.* Burlington, Vt.: Vermont Student Assistance Corporation, 1975.

Historical summary and report on four state programs: incentive grants, guaranteed student loans, talent search, and honor scholarships. Includes statistical appendixes.

III.L.25. West Virginia Scholarship Program. *Annual report, 1973–1974.* Charleston, W. Va.: West Virginia State Legislature, 1974.

Describes the history and operation of the program, including a statistical description of award recipients.

III.L.26. Woodrow Wilson National Fellowship Foundation. *Reports for 1972–73, 1973–74.* Princeton, N.J.: Woodrow Wilson National Fellowship Foundation, 1975.

A description of the programs and services of the foundation.

IV. Financial Aid Administration as a Profession

For many years, financial aid programs were administered as a part-time function of a senior college official. This was possible because aid programs and recipients were few and the tasks of aid administration did not require full-time attention. But because the programs were always considered important, they were generally administered by high-ranking officers, usually the president.

With the expansion of federal, state, and institutional aid programs following World War II, aid administration became a full-time occupation. At the same time, programs became more complex. The diversity of policies and practices and the use of need analysis systems required that aid administrators develop special sets of skills to perform their duties. Thus, the financial aid profession came into being.

The items cited in this chapter relate to the financial aid profession. The chapter is divided into three sections: characteristics of aid administrators, training and professional development, and activities of professional associations.

IV. A. Characteristics of Aid Administrators

The first nationwide study of the characteristics and functions of college financial aid administrators was conducted by the Columbia University Bureau of Applied Social Research (Nash and Lazarsfeld, 1965). This study serves as a bench mark for later research on the development of the profession.

Many of the subsequent studies have been doctoral dissertations. Moore (1969) studies the personality characteristics and academic preparation of aid administrators. Casazza (1970, 1971) focuses attention on the educational backgrounds and career patterns of administrators at larger colleges and universities. Casazza's study was later replicated by Maddox (1976).

Gedney (1972) studies the characteristics and functions of administrators at community colleges in Virginia; Barry (1974) identifies characteristics of high-ranking aid administrators on campuses in the Midwest; and Heath (1976) presents career profiles of aid administrators at institutions in the Big Eight area. An earlier study by Whitis (1972) describes the roles of aid administrators in the western states. Herndon (1972) compares the views of students, presidents, and aid administrators on the professional competency of aid administrators at 45 California community colleges.

In addition to these dissertations, three other studies are cited. Chambers (1972) and Puryear (1974) identify characteristics of aid administrators at institutions in the South. Schiesz (1974) reports on the career patterns of administrators in Illinois. The need for a better understanding of personal attitudes and characteristics of aid administrators is discussed in an article by Hinko (1971).

The literature demonstrates that aid administrators have varied, and frequently rich, backgrounds. Most hold master's degrees and many have doctorates. While they come from many different academic backgrounds, the majority have had training in business, the social and behavioral sciences, and in student personnel activities. The studies indicate that most aid administrators have held their present positions for a relatively short period of time (less than five years). As the demand for trained aid administrators increases, the average tenures are increasing. The majority of aid administrators are content with their jobs and many will use them as stepping-stones to higher administrative positions in postsecondary institutions.

IV.A.1. Barry, J. G. *A study of the role of the director of financial aid in his own institution in selected colleges and universities in the Midwest.* Chicago, Ill.: Loyola University of Chicago, 1974. (Dissertation)

Surveys 150 aid administrators to determine which of several selected factors related to the importance of the administrator on the campus. High ranking administrators were male, had doctorates or were in doctoral programs, and were involved in the profession as leaders in financial aid workshops.

IV.A.2. Casazza, C. L. *Career patterns of financial aid directors.* Bloomington, Ind.: Indiana University, 1970. (Dissertation)

Surveys the educational backgrounds, career patterns, and career plans of aid administrators at colleges with enrollments of 10,000 or more. Reports that the majority are satisfied with their work and careers.

IV.A.3. Casazza, C. L. Career patterns of financial aid directors. *Journal of Student Financial Aid,* Vol. 1, November 1971, pp. 33–40.

Reports on the career progression and aspirations of financial aid directors at 131 colleges and universities with enrollments of 10,000 or more students.

IV.A.4. Chambers, O. W. *A survey of the professional development of student financial aid administrators in nine southern states.* Nashville, Tenn.: Southern Association of Student Financial Aid Administrators, 1972.

Reports on a 1971 survey of the professional development, academic background, professional characteristics, and needs for future development of aid administrators at 433 colleges and universities. Respondents indicated a need for graduate programs in aid administration, training workshops and programs, and education of their faculties and administrators on the role of financial aid administrators in campus development.

IV.A.5. Gedney, E. C. *A study of selected characteristics and functions of financial aid officers within the Virginia community college system.* Charlottesville, Va.: University of Virginia, 1972. (Dissertation)

Survey of 21 aid administrators at 18 colleges. Found that typical aid administrator is male, 33 years of age, married, Protestant, a Democrat, has a master's degree, has been in aid work less than two years, and does not teach or have tenure.

IV.A.6. Heath, H. E. *A career profile and an investigation into the financial aid practices of financial aid directors in the Big Eight area.* Lincoln, Nebr.: University of Nebraska, 1976. (Dissertation)

Survey of the age, sex, educational status, and employment history of 46 campus-based aid administrators. Found that over 90 percent were satisfied with their work and viewed it as both a lifelong career alternative and preparation for other administrative positions.

IV.A.7. Herndon, C. F. *Comparative perceptions of students, financial aid administrators, and presidents regarding the required competencies of community college financial aid administrators.* Corvallis, Oreg.: Oregon State University, 1972. (Dissertation)

Studies the views of student aid recipients, college presidents, and aid administrators at 45 California community colleges on the professional competencies required of the aid administrator. Describes implications of study fundings for training of aid administrators.

IV.A.8. Hinko, P. M. Financial aid officers and institutional programs. *Junior College Journal,* Vol. 41, April 1971, pp. 20-23.

Advocates a need for better understanding of personal attitudes and characteristics of institutional financial aid administrators.

IV.A.9. Maddox, M. M. *Career patterns of chief student financial aid administrators.* Bloomington, Ind.: Indiana University, 1976. (Dissertation)

Essentially a replication of the 1970 Casazza survey study of administrators at colleges of 10,000 or more students. Based on responses from 140 persons.

IV.A.10. Moore, S. B. *Personality characteristics and preparation of financial aid administrators.* Port Collins, Colo.: Colorado State University, 1969. (Dissertation)

Describes the kinds of coursework successful aid administrators believe essential for preparation in their field. Most important are courses dealing with aid office operational procedures.

IV.A.11. Nash, G. The current status of financial aid administration. *National ACAC Journal,* Vol. 13, September 1968, pp. 5-8.

Discusses strengths and weaknesses in the occupational status of college aid administrators as revealed in data collected from national surveys. Provides useful background data on the development of the profession.

IV.A.12. Nash, G. and Lazarsfeld, P. F. *New administrator on campus: A study of the director of student financial aid.* New York: Bureau of Applied Social Research, Columbia University, 1965. (Mimeographed)

Reports on an extensive national survey of the financial aid profession, backgrounds of aid administrators, and the organization of the profession in higher education.

IV.A.13. Puryear, J. B. Two-year college financial aid offices. *Journal of College Student Personnel,* Vol. 15, January 1974, pp. 12–16.

Describes the characteristics, responsibilities, and activities of two-year college aid administrators in the southern states.

IV.A.14. Schiesz, R. J. A study of certain professional characteristics of financial aid administrators at institutions of higher education in the state of Illinois. *Journal of Student Financial Aid,* Vol. 4, March 1974, pp. 25–33.

Survey of career patterns, amount and type of training, methods employed to insure professional competence, professional activities, and judgments concerning avenues for achieving professional status of financial aid administrators.

IV.A.15. Whitis, J. D. *A study of the leadership role of financial aid officers of the Western Association of Financial Aid Officers.* Tempe, Ariz.: Arizona State University, 1972. (Dissertation)

Compares the real and ideal leadership behavior of financial aid administrators in the areas of Consideration and Initiating Structure.

IV.B. Training and Professional Development

Studies on the characteristics of aid administrators reveal a need for more training in the area of professional skills. As administrators accept a wider range of duties and responsibilities, this training will become vital.

Several items in this section offer suggestions about the kinds of training needed and how that training can be obtained. Willingham's (1970) survey of aid administrators in the West is one of the earliest references in this area. Moore (1971) suggests a series of courses for aid administrators and Delaney, et al. (1974) provide a taxonomy of training objectives. Carr (1975) proposes a master's degree program for aid administrators. In his dissertation, Bryan (1972) tested the effects of a short-term training program.

One method of training which has proved useful for new administrators is internship in aid offices. Johnson (1972) and Morris (1972) report on internship programs at two different colleges.

Fields (1976) is concerned with the financial aid training of high school guidance counselors. He reports on a survey of the types of financial aid training these persons receive in graduate school programs.

The large increase in personnel concerned with the performance of financial aid activities has led to a concern for professionalization and certification. Sanderson (1971) sets forth the need for professionalization in an early article in *The Journal of Student Financial Aid*. Moore (1975) challenges the certification criteria established by the National Association of Student Financial Aid Administrators.

IV. B. 1. Bryan, C. *The impact of a short term training program for financial aid administrators and other student assistance personnel.* Pocatello, Idaho: Idaho State University, 1972. (Dissertation)

Study of the attitudinal and behavioral effects of a short-term training program on 33 aid administrators of varied experience and background.

IV. B. 2. Carr, J. W. *A proposed master's program of studies for student financial aid administrators.* Tallahassee, Fla.: Florida State University, 1975. (Dissertation)

Using data from a survey of aid administrator perceptions and observations of needed training and observations from a panel of aid experts, the author recommends a 50 quarter-hour program of study. The program contains courses in educational finance, computers, college law, business management, and statistics.

IV. B. 3. Delaney, F. H., Jr., et al. A taxonomy of objectives for the training of financial aid administrators. *Journal of Student Financial Aid,* Vol. 4, November 1974, pp. 5–12.

Taxonomy of training objectives in three major areas: social sciences, administrative and organizational studies, and behavioral sciences. Suggests courses on topical areas of concern which should be included in a training program.

IV. B. 4. Fields, C. R. Financial aid training for high school counselors. *Journal of Student Financial Aid,* Vol. 6, November 1976, pp. 33–38.

Reports on a survey of types of financial aid training received by graduate students in counselor training programs at 191 colleges and universities. Offers a sample course outline for the training of high school counselors.

IV. B. 5. Johnson, B. G. Mini-internships – A method for professional improvement, orientation, and recruitment. *Journal of Student Financial Aid,* Vol. 2, May 1972, pp. 19–22.

Describes the program of mini-internships on student aid for graduate students in student personnel work at Texas A&M University.

IV. B. 6. Moore, D. R. Certification of financial aid professionals. *Journal of Student Financial Aid,* Vol. 5, November 1975, pp. 15–20.

Challenges the criteria for the certification of aid administrators developed by the National Association of Student Financial Aid Administrators. Suggests basic competencies on which certification should be based.

IV. B. 7. Moore, S. B. Suggested courses for the preparation of financial aid administrators. *Journal of College Student Personnel,* Vol. 12, March 1971, pp. 143–146.

Describes the kinds of courses successful aid administrators feel are essential for professional preparation. Most important are courses dealing with operational procedures.

IV. B. 8. Morris, T. D. A report on the financial aid internship program at the California State College, Fullerton. *Journal of Student Financial Aid,* Vol. 2, March 1972, pp. 35–40.

Describes the development, operation, financing, and curriculum of the internship program at California State College.

IV. B. 9. Sanderson, J. R. Why professionalization for financial aid officers? *Journal of Student Financial Aid,* Vol. 1, May 1971, pp. 7–13.

Discusses the meaning of professionalism and the need for professional development of financial aid administrators. Suggests some initial steps to encourage and achieve professionalism.

IV. B. 10. Willingham, W. W. *Professional development of financial aid officers.* Higher Education Surveys Report No. 2. New York: College Entrance Examination Board, 1970.

Study of the professional development of aid administrators, their training needs, and their attitudes about professional development. Based on a survey of administrators at 122 western colleges and universities. Contains a series of recommendations for training and professional development.

IV.C. Activities of Professional Associations

The growth of the financial aid profession has led to the development of several professional associations. These include associations of administrators in each state; large regional associations, such as the Eastern Association of Student Financial Aid Administrators and its counterparts in the South, West, and Midwest; and national organizations, such as the National Association of Student Financial Aid Administrators, the National Association of State Scholarship and Grant Programs, the National Council on Higher Education Loan Programs, and the College Scholarship Service Assembly. There are also associations representing particular interests and concerns, such as the Midwest Association of Student Employment Directors and the National Association of Financial Aids for Minority Students.

Professional associations play an important role in the financial aid professions. They provide forums for the continued discussion and resolution of problems and issues in student aid and educational financing; they articulate the interests of their members to federal and state governments and to the public; and they offer training and professional development activities for their members. Yet, aside from their training and development activities, professional associations have received little attention in the literature of student aid. Only one item on associations and their activities is cited here.

The activities of associations deserve systematic analysis, particularly because they influence the policies and practices of student aid and indirectly affect the ways in which aid is distributed among and delivered to students. Further study is needed on the ways in which associations choose to promote various policy alternatives; the extent to which these policy positions represent their memberships' interests and the interests of students, institutions, and society; and the influence of association activities. Reports on the similar activities of labor unions and other professional organizations such as the American Medical Association exist in the literature of political science. These studies might serve as models for future studies on the role of the professional association in the structure and function of the financial aid system.

IV.C.1. Parish. H. C. Professional associations—Genesis and development. In *Money, marbles, or chalk: Student financial support in higher education.* Keene, R., Adams, F. C., and King, J. E. (Eds.) Carbondale, Ill.: Southern Illinois University Press, 1975.

Discusses the early history and development of aid administrators' associations and some of their current activities.

V. Federal and State Issues and Problems in Student Aid

Under the United States Constitution, it is the responsibility of the states to provide for the education of their citizens. The states exercise this responsibility with regard to postsecondary education by appropriating funds to establish and operate institutions and support financial aid programs which help students pay for the costs of education. Although the states still provide the largest amount of financial support to postsecondary education, the federal government, in the general public interest, has gradually increased its role and contributions. Federal contributions are made through special purpose and categorical grants and loans to institutions and through direct financial aid to students.

Providing resources to fund student aid programs is now considered an appropriately shared responsibility of the state and federal governments. The funding of aid programs has gradually evolved into a "partnership" among the governments, the postsecondary institutions themselves and, to a lesser extent, the private sectors of the economy. Because the federal and state governments provide nearly 90 percent of all financial aid funds awarded to students, their roles in the partnership are especially significant.

The items identified in this chapter are primarily concerned with the issues and problems related to the ways in which the student aid partnership functions. Many of these issues can reasonably be described as federal or state, or both federal and state issues because of the large role these partners play in providing aid to students.

The partnership in student aid is considered appropriate not only because of shared responsibilities for funding aid programs and educating students, but because of shared interests in the goals of financial aid programs and their product, that is, a trained, educated, and skilled citizenry. A collection of papers published by the Association of American Colleges (1974) contains useful background data on the relationship of higher education to the national economy and the public welfare. A review of these papers will provide readers with an understanding of the philosophies underlying support of postsecondary institutions and their students. Elaborations on the partnership concept, and suggestions for improving its structure and function, are contained in three items (Boyd, 1971; Bureau of Postsecondary Education, 1974; Task Force on Student Assistance, 1971).

The federal government's role in financing students and institutions is the subject of a collection of papers (Orwig, 1971) and of documents by

Trotter (1975) and Conrad and Cosand (1976). Three items are concerned with the role of the federal government in support of specific groups of students (Green, 1975; Quie, 1973; Ross, 1975). A Carnegie Commission (1972) report proposes a specific federal role through a coordinated system of support to institutions.

Federal legislation and its implications form the topic of several references. Three items examine various proposals before Congress in the early 1970s (Gladieux, 1972; Pell, 1971; Saunders, 1971). Boyd (1972) and Young (1973) discuss the student aid implications of the Higher Education Amendments Act of 1972. Hogan (1973b) examines the potential impact of the Basic Educational Opportunity Grants Program, which was created by that act, on the structure of student support from various sources. Three documents deal with recent amendments to Title IV of the 1972 Act (Consortium on Financing Higher Education, 1975; Gladieux, 1975; U.S. Congress, House Committee on Education and Labor, 1975).

A perennial concern among many educators is that federal involvement in support of higher education will infringe on institutional autonomy. Finn (1975-76) and Quie (1975) expound their concerns on this matter. Hogan (1973a) believes that recent congressional legislation on student aid favors institutional autonomy. A study by El-Khawas and Kinzer (1974) shows how federal financial aid policies have in fact, affected institutional policies. Ford (1972) focuses attention on the constitutional and legal implications of federal aid to higher education.

Another prominent issue concerning federal aid programs is the way in which their policies and practices are coordinated. Two studies of this problem offer suggestions for better coordination (Comptroller General of the United States, 1972; Phillips, et al., 1973). Lee, et al., (1975) and Hershberger (1975) report the results of a national analysis of the effects of federal financial aid policies on the distribution of aid among students and institutions. Three other studies deal with the management and operation of federal programs that support students enrolled in health professions programs (MacBride, 1973a, 1973b; U.S. Congress, 1976).

The state's role in financing postsecondary education is discussed by Kirkpatrick (1971). Mathews (1974) examines this role with respect to student aid programs, A Southern Regional Education Board (1973) report describes state student aid activities in the South. Boyd (1975) and Holderman (1975) discuss the philosophies, planning, and management of state-supported student aid programs.

Two issues cutting across state and federal levels have received attention in recent years. The first concerns the system by which private agency accreditation of institutions is used to determine whether postsecondary institutions and their students are eligible to receive funds from public sources. The issue is whether the standards of a nongovernmental agency should be employed by governmental agencies. The system of private accreditation, its use by public agencies, and its policy implications are discussed in two studies (Institute for Educational Leadership, 1975; Orlans, et al., 1974).

The second issue concerns the public colleges' practice of charging higher tuitions for nonresidents of the states in which they are located. It is believed that this practice may be illegal (Palley, 1976) or, at the very least, unfair because it reduces interstate migration of students, thereby potentially inhibiting student access and choice among colleges. The practice of charging higher tuitions for nonresidents is justified by the rationale that residents' taxes pay for the direct subsidies of public institutions and nonresidents' taxes do not. However, since institutions also receive support from the federal government through federal taxes, some policymakers argue that nonresidents' taxes do, in fact, contribute to institutional support. Carbone (1970, 1973, 1974, 1975) discusses these issues and offers predictions about their resolution.

One of the most controversial financial aid issues in recent years is that of public support of private colleges and their students. Because of their higher tuitions, private institutions are at a disadvantage in the student marketplace and, therefore, find themselves in difficult financial circumstances. It is argued that these institutions serve a vital national role in providing access and choice to students and that they and their students should receive public support. Although many policymakers agree that private colleges and their students should be assisted, there is little consensus on the types or amounts of assistance they should receive.

Three items provide useful discussions of the various philosophical, legal, and political issues concerning public support of private colleges and their students (Berdahl, 1970; McFarlane, 1973; McFarlane and Wheeler, 1971). Abrahams and Schweppe (1970) report on a national survey of state practices in support of private higher education. More recent surveys of this type are reported by McFarlane, Howard, and Chronister (1974) and Millard and Berve (1975). All provide excellent data on policies and practices in each state. Garner (1974) recommends a program of state support for private colleges and students in Massachusetts and the National Council of Independent Colleges and Universities (1974) asserts that modest changes in public policy could alleviate the financial problems of private institutions.

A variety of other matters are discussed in the references listed here. Willingham (1970) and Ferrin (1971) describe the availability of free-access institutions (that is, low-cost, conveniently located colleges with relatively open admissions requirements) in each state.

Honey and Hartle (1975) and Nicolette (1974) describe voucher or entitlement aid program proposals which the authors believe could solve many student aid problems. A voucher program provides students with government-supported vouchers that pay for a fixed amount of educational services. Generally, these vouchers are intended to be used as institutional income in lieu of tax-supported tuition subsidies to colleges.

Newell (1970) presents a tuition plan for talented poor students. Nies (1974) reports on why women receive disproportionately fewer fellowships than men and makes recommendations for increasing fellowships to women.

Some financial aid programs provide student loans which do not have to be repaid if the student obtains employment in a specified occupation or geographic region after graduation. These are sometimes called "scholarship-loans" because they are scholarships for those students who meet the employment criteria but are loans for those who do not. Boe (1974) and Eglick (1974) discuss the treatment of these types of awards under the IRS Code.

V.1. Abrahams, L. and Schweppe, L. *A limited study of the status of state support of private higher education.* Washington, D.C.: Academy for Educational Development, 1970.

Reports on state support for private higher education: the mechanisms employed, the current program appropriations, and state aid to students in private institutions. Describes recently proposed legislation and action in these areas.

V.2. Assocation of American Colleges. *Higher education, human resources and the national economy: Addresses and discussion papers from the sixtieth annual meeting of the Association of American Colleges,* 1974.

Collection of 21 papers on the relationship between higher education—its organization, policies, and practices—and the nation's economy.

V.3. Berdahl, R. D. Private higher education and state governments. *Educational Record,* Vol. 51, Summer 1970, pp. 285–295.

Because state relations with higher education are increasingly important, the author believes that some important questions should be answered: How will public interests be adequately protected? Is state aid to church-related institutions constitutional? What roles will statewide coordinating agencies play in any new system?

V.4. Bloustein, E. J. Higher education at the crossroads. *Planning for Higher Education,* Vol. 5, April 1976, pp. 4–5.

Suggests that the ultimate goal of public policy should be to eliminate tuition for higher education.

V. 5. Boe, C. C. Cancelled student loans: For the benefit of the grantor? *Albany Law Review*, Vol. 39, No. 1, 1974, pp. 35–51.

Discusses the treatment of scholarships and fellowships under the Internal Revenue Code and court interpretations of them. Concludes that there is a need for amendments to the code.

V. 6. Boyd, J. D. A federal/state/institutional partnership in providing opportunity grants for financially needy students. *Journal of Student Financial Aid*, Vol. 1, November 1971, pp. 28–32.

Presents the position paper of the National Association of State Scholarship Programs with regard to the partnership in financial aid. Describes the potential effects of funding and adoption of the position on aid administration.

V. 7. Boyd, J. D. Education amendments of 1972: Positive impact or days of tension? *Financial Aid Report*, Vol. 2, November 1972.

Examines several aspects of the new law that might affect state aid institutions.

V. 8. Boyd, J. D. State programs of financial aid. In *Money, marbles, or chalk: Student financial support in higher education*. Keene, R., Adams, F. C., and King, J. E. (Eds.) Carbondale, Ill.: Southern Illinois University Press, 1975.

Offers some suggestions for the planning of state aid programs in coordination with other public aid programs.

V. 9. Bureau of Postsecondary Education. *Institutional-state-federal partnership in student assistance: Final recommendations of the national work conference*. Washington, D.C.: U.S. Office of Education, 1974.

Series of recommendations concerning the administration, management, and coordination of federal, state, and institutional student aid programs.

V. 10. Carbone, R. F. *Alternative tuition systems. Special report twelve*. Iowa City, Iowa: American College Testing Program, 1974.

Describes five alternative models to current differential tuition policies at public institutions. Analyzes legal, economic, political, and educational implications of each model.

V. 11. Carbone, R. F. Is the nonresident student being treated fairly? *College Board Review*, No. 76, Summer 1970, pp. 22–24.

Believes that nonresident tuition charges at public colleges inhibit student access and discriminate against substantial numbers of students. Suggests that interstate exchange programs and reciprocal agreements be adopted to remove differential charges.

V. 12. Carbone, R. F. Public college tuition flap. *Saturday Review*, February 8, 1975, pp. 49–50.

Briefly discusses the conflict between higher tuition charges to out-of-state students and new 18-year-old adulthood laws. Believes that students might be encouraged to flock to states with richer financial aid programs.

V. 13. Carbone, R. G. *Students and state borders.* Special report No. 7. Iowa City, Iowa: American College Testing Program, 1973.

Discusses nonresident student status regulations and other current barriers to student migration, including admissions quotas, differential admissions standards, and tuition policies.

V. 14. Carnegie Commission on Higher Education. *Institutional aid—Federal support to colleges and universities.* New York: McGraw-Hill, 1972.

Report on the need for direct federal aid to institutions. Proposes a variegated system of cost of education supplements—funds for construction, for research, for special programs such as health, and for institutional grants.

V. 15. Comptroller General of the United States. *Need for improved coordination of federally assisted student aid programs in institutions of higher education.* Washington, D.C.: U.S. General Accounting Office, 1972.

Examination of the coordination of federal need-based programs on college campuses. Recommends that HEW require institutions to provide for coordination procedures on their campuses.

V. 16. Conrad, C. and Cosand, J. *The implications of federal education policy.* Washington, D.C.: American Association for Higher Education, 1976.

Critical review of current federal policy on providing equal educational opportunity and maintaining the quality of postsecondary education. Suggests new directions for identifying and implementing federal policies.

V. 17. Consortium on Financing Higher Education. *Federal student assistance: A review of Title IV of the Higher Education Act.* Hanover, N.H.: Consortium on Financing Higher Education, 1975.

Proposes a financial aid structure involving redirection of benefits under existing laws to provide students with access and choice.

V. 18. Dellenback, J. *Financial aid to independent students at the postsecondary level: The federal government's role.* Speech, 1974. (ERIC ED 091953, HE 005394)

Suggests changes in the Basic Educational Opportunity Grants and College Work-Study programs to help aid independent students.

V. 19. Eglick, P. J. Taxation of forgiven student loans. *Georgetown Law Journal,* Vol. 62, March 1974, pp. 1243–1260.

Discusses issues concerning the tax status of scholarships and fellowship grants.

V. 20. El-Khawas, E. H. and Kinzer, J. L. *The impact of Office of Education student assistance programs, Fall 1973.* Higher Education Panel Reports, No. 18. Washington, D.C.: American Council on Education, 1974.

Reports on a 1973 survey of 515 two-year and four-year colleges to determine the impact of Office of Education student assistance programs on institutional policies. In general, the results indicate that the programs had little effect on admissions and tuition policies, but a far greater impact on recruiting policies, the overall financial condition of the institution, student counseling, and other sources of student support.

V.21. Ferrin, R. I. *A decade of change in free-access higher education.* New York: College Entrance Examination Board, 1971.

Supplements Willingham's *Free-Access Higher Education* by providing comparable data on institutional accessibility for 1958 and 1968. Permits a description of patterns of change as well as factors contributing to them.

V.22. Finn, C. E., Jr. Federalism and the universities. The balance shifts. *Change,* Vol. 7, December–January 1975–1976, pp. 24–29.

Notes that higher education has made decisions on behalf of government through accreditation, private need analysis systems, and peer review of institutional allocations. Calls for reform of higher education management to preserve institutional autonomy.

V.23. Ford, W. D. The constitutional implications of federal aid to higher education. *Journal of Law and Education,* Vol. 1, October 1972, pp. 513–540.

Analyzes the implications of aid to higher education, focusing attention on the *Massachusetts* v. *Mellon* and the *Tilton* v. *Richardson* cases.

V.24. Garner, L. *State aid to private colleges and universities.* Cambridge, Mass.: Task Force on Massachusetts Higher Education, Harvard University, 1974.

Study found that private institutions in Massachusetts contribute to the achievement of access and choice and to educational diversity but access is not equally provided. Private colleges provide greater access and choice to high-income students from urban areas. Believes that lack of increased state aid to private institutions will, in the near future, inhibit access, choice, and diversity. Recommends a program of increased state student aid and direct grants to private students and institutions.

V.25. Gladieux, L. A perspective on federal student aid legislation. *Financial Aid Report,* Vol. 1, May 1972.

Analyzes federal student aid legislation before Congress, the differences in Senate and House proposals, and the central question of priorities in federal assistance.

V.26. Gladieux, L. E. *Federal student aid programs: A comparison of legislative options.* New York: College Entrance Examination Board, 1975.

Summarizes the positions of interested parties on extension and amendment of Title IV of the Higher Education Act.

V.27. Glenny, L. A. Nine myths, nine realities: The illusion of steady state. *Change,* Vol. 6, December–January 1974–75, pp. 24–28.
Describes popular conceptions and misunderstandings concerning the steady state in higher education.

V.28. Green, E. The future is now. *College and University,* Vol. 51, Fall 1975, pp. 5–16.
Congresswoman discusses her opposition to aid programs which support the children of poor families at the expense of middle-income families.

V.29. Herschberger, A. M. *The development of the data base for student aid: Descriptions and options.* Menlo Park, Calif.: Stanford Research Institute, 1975.
Describes the problems involved in development and organization of data in student aid research. These include: obtaining data from different sources that categorize data differently; preparing estimates to account for missing data; resolving disparities in data reported by different sources; and formulating useful categories for analysis.

V.30. Hogan, H. J. Student aid and institutional autonomy: Congressional decisions. *Journal of Student Financial Aid,* Vol. 3, March 1973a, pp. 5–18.
Discusses, on a program-by-program basis, the impact on institutional autonomy, of the 1972 amendments to federal student aid programs. Concludes that there is a consistent congressional intent to favor the autonomy of institutions.

V.31. Hogan, H. J. The Basic Educational Opportunity Grant Program: Its impact on the middle class. *Journal of Student Fiancial Aid,* Vol. 3, June 1973b, pp. 19–26.
Critical analysis of the potential effects of BEOG legislation on the structure of family, state, and federal support to students and institutions. Believes the program will have a greater impact on middle-class than on lower-class students and families.

V.32. Holderman, J. B. State coordination and student support. In *Money, marbles, or chalk: Student financial support in higher education.* Keene, R., Adams, F. C., and King, J. E. (Eds.) Carbondale, Ill.: Southern Illinois University Press, 1975.
Believes that the subsidization of students through financial aid programs to meet higher instructional costs represents a more effective use of limited dollars than providing direct subsidies to colleges.

V.33. Honey, J. C. and Hartle, T. W. *A career education entitlement plan: Administrative and political issues.* Syracuse, N.Y.: Educational Finance and Governance Center, Syracuse University Research Corporation, 1975.
Examines administrative and political issues of various educational entitlement and voucher plans for postsecondary education. Proposes a new program based on existing entitlement programs.

V.34. Institute for Educational Leadership. *Report on institutional eligibility.* Washington, D.C.: George Washington University, 1975.

Report on the implications of accreditation of institutions by private agencies for determination of eligibility to receive public funds.

V. 35. Kirkpatrick, J. I. Financing higher education: The role of the state. *College Board Review,* No. 79, Spring 1971, pp. 22-25.

Discusses who should pay for higher education: the state, parents, or students.

V. 36. Lee, J. B., et al. *Student aid: Descriptions and options.* Menlo Park, Calif.: Educational Policy Research Center, Stanford Research Institute, 1975.

Describes how federal, state, and institutional aid is distributed among students by states, types of institutions, and family incomes. Discusses a linear model that simulates the distribution of student aid under different legislation and appropriation levels.

V. 37. MacBride, O. *An overview of the Health Professions Educational Assistance Act, 1963-1971.* Report No. A1, 1973a. (ERIC ED 11245, HE 006609)

Reviews the history of health professions aid to institutions and students.

V. 38. MacBride, O. *Legislative history of the federal formula-grant program under the Health Professions Educational Assistance Act, 1963-1971. Report No. A2, 1973b.* (ERIC ED 11244, HE 006608)

Reviews legislation regarding federal assistance to the health professions since 1963, including support to students and institutions. Notes that institutions have regarded awards as subsidies to existing programs and not incentives to increase enrollments.

V. 39. Mathews, J. The states move in on student aid. *Compact,* Vol. 8, May-June 1974, pp. 23-27.

Discusses the student aid debate in Congress and the rising importance of state student aid programs.

V. 40. McFarlane, W. H. State aid for Virginia's private colleges? *Journal of Law and Education,* Vol. 2, October 1973, pp. 593-621.

A case study describing the difficulties in developing a private college subsidy program that responds to institutional needs, political considerations, and legal constraints.

V. 41. McFarlane, W. H., Howard, A. E. D., and Chronister, J. L. *State financial measures involving the private sector of higher education.* Washington, D.C.: National Council of Independent Colleges and Universities, 1974.

Examines state aid to the private sector of higher education in terms of constitutional limitations, programmatic details, and evidence of impacts. Special attention is given to recurrent patterns indicating policy trends of national significance. Provides extensive data on student aid to private colleges.

V. 42. McFarlane, W. H. and Wheeler, C. L. Views on state aid to private colleges: Summary of legal and political issues of state aid to private higher education. *School and Society,* Vol. 99, October 1971, pp. 325-327.

Looks at broader questions concerning limitations, strategies, and impacts of state programs of support for private higher education.

V.43. Millard, R. M. and Berve, N. M. *The states and higher education.* Denver, Colo.: Education Commission of the States, 1975.

Tabular survey of state programs that support private education in each of the 50 states.

V.44. National Council of Independent Colleges and Universities. *A national policy for private higher education. The report of a task force of the National Council of Independent Colleges and Universities.* Washington, D.C.: Association of American Colleges, 1974.

Argues that financial problems of private higher education could be alleviated with modest changes in public policy. Emphasizes tuition equalization grants for students at private colleges.

V.45. Newell, B. W. Enter now and pay later. *Educational Record,* Vol. 51, Winter 1970, pp. 57–59.

Recommends a new tuition plan for talented but financially poor high school graduates.

V.46. Nicolette, J. R. *Voucher plans for student financial aid awards in higher education: Critique and appraisal.* Albany, N.Y.: State University of New York, 1974. (Dissertation)

Discusses the consistency of current need analysis systems in determining expected contributions; whether existing aid programs can be reduced to one basic federal grant, one basic state grant, and one loan with no interest benefits or income limitations; and whether a voucher system would be more effective in eliminating inequities of awards procedures.

V.47. Nies, J. *Women and fellowships.* Washington, D.C.: Women's Equity Action League, 1974.

Reports on the reasons women receive disproportionately fewer fellowships than men. Offers recommendations to increase greater fellowship participation by women.

V.48. Ohio Board of Regents. *Expanding opportunities for equal access to higher education for Ohioans: A report on the Ohio Instructional Grants Program.* Columbus, Ohio: Ohio Board of Regents, 1975.

Reviews the history and experiences of the Ohio Instructional Grants Program. Concludes that the program merits high priority but must be modified to increase access and choice in Ohio. Recommends a series of modifications.

V.49. Orlans, H., et al. *Private accreditation and public eligibility, Vols. 1 and 2.* Washington, D.C.: Office of Planning, Budgeting, and Evaluation, 1974.

Reports on an HEW-funded study on the use of private accreditation to establish eligibility of postsecondary institutions for aid from federal programs.

V.50. Orwig, M. D. (Ed.) *Financing higher education: Alternatives for the federal government,* Iowa City, Iowa: American College Testing Program, 1971.

Collection of papers dealing with major problems and proposals most frequently cited in discussion of financing higher education. Includes a bibliography.

V.51. Palley, D. G. Resolving the nonresident student problem: Two federal proposals. *Journal of Higher Education,* Vol. 47, January-February 1976, pp. 1-31.

Discusses the interstate migration barriers of tuition, financial aid, and admissions policies and analyzes courses open to states after a Supreme Court decision concerning 18-year-old adulthood. Describes two different plans, the Transfer Payment Plan and the Fee Waiver Plan.

V.52. Pell, C. Education amendments of 1971. *Journal of Student Financial Aid,* Vol. 1, November 1971, pp. 18-21.

Discussion by a U.S. Senator of his proposal to amend federal student aid legislation.

V.53. Phillips, J., et al. DHEW/USOE *task force on management of student assistance programs: Preliminary report to the deputy commissioner for higher education.* Washington, D.C.: U.S. Office of Education, 1973.

Reviews the management of ten federal student assistance programs. Discusses policy issues, program objectives, coordination of management functions and resources, costs and benefits, and legislative alternatives for improved management.

V.54. Quie, A. H. Legislation for the new Congress. *Community and Junior College Journal,* Vol. 45, March 1975, pp. 30-31.

Discusses various forms of federal and state student aid. The author is concerned that increased aid to institutions would lead to increased intervention in institutional operations.

V.55. Quie, A. H. *Remarks on the federal role, education and teacher education.* Lincoln, Nebr.: University of Nebraska, 1973.

Discusses implications of current events and federal policy changes on colleges and the education of teachers.

V.56. Ross, J. The role of federal financial aid in equalizing educational opportunity. *National ACAC Journal,* Vol. 19, March 1975, pp. 13-16.

Discusses the need for better coordination of federal financial aid programs and Upward Bound, Talent Search, and Special Services programs. Believes the federal government should exercise greater responsibility in removing educational barriers for minority/poverty students.

V.57. Saunders, H. R. The administration's student aid proposals. *Journal of Student Financial Aid,* Vol. 1, May 1971, pp. 28-33.

Supports the Nixon administration's student aid proposals.

V.58. Southern Regional Education Board. *Student financial aid in the South, Number 25, Financing higher education.* Atlanta: Southern Regional Education Board, 1973.

Brief report on the costs of education and aid available to help students meet those costs in southern states in 1972–1973. Gives special emphasis to ways that state-sponsored programs function to help meet student aid needs.

V.59. State Department of Education. *A report on constituent involvement in decision-making: The forum on financial assistance. Financial assistance for postsecondary education. Working note No. 5.* Providence, R.I.: Bureau of Postsecondary Education, Rhode Island State Department of Education, 1974.

Reports on pre- and post-conference ranking of importance of criteria for use in selecting financial aid recipients.

V.60. Task Force on Student Assistance. *Postsecondary educational opportunity: A federal-state-institutional partnership.* Denver, Colo.: Education Commission of the States, 1971.

Final report and recommendations of the ECS task force. Delineates the separate and interrelated roles of states, institutions, and the federal government in providing a comprehensive program of student assistance to increase equality of access and choice in postsecondary education.

V.61. Trotter, V. Y. Bicentennial perspective on education. *College and University,* Vol. 50, Summer 1975, pp. 626–632.

Discusses federal policies and goals for higher education.

V.62. U.S. Congress. *The role of aid to medical, osteopathic, and dental students in a new health manpower education policy. Staff working paper.* Washington, D.C.: Government Printing Office, 1976.

Discusses current and future financial aid to medical, osteopathic, and dental students within the context of federal manpower objectives. Various options are described.

V.63. U.S. Congress, House Committee on Education and Labor. *The student financial aid act of 1975. Hearings before the Subcommittee on Postsecondary Education of the Committee on Labor.* Washington, D.C.: Government Printing Office, 1975.

Discussion of the student financial aid amendments to Title IV of the Higher Education Act of 1975.

V.64. Willingham, W. W. *Free-access higher education.* New York: College Entrance Examination Board, 1970.

State-by-state analysis of the availability of free-access institutions. Profiles each state with data and tabular information to describe the availability of institutions and who can benefit from them.

V.65. Young, K. E. A new order. Implications for higher education of the higher education amendments of 1972. *College and University Journal,* Vol. 12, January 1973, pp. 4–8.

Believes the most important aspects of the act are: upgrading education within HEW; creation of the National Institute of Education; creation of the Fund for Support for Improvement of Postsecondary Education; and establishment of the principle of institutional aid.

VI. Financial Aid and Financing Postsecondary Education

Although the administration of financial aid programs primarily concerns student financing, the patterns of student finance directly affect the financing of institutions.

The types and amounts of resources available to students and where those resources are spent have a direct bearing on institutional financing. Without students and without tuitions, institutions could not survive. This is true whether the tuitions are defrayed by financial aid resources or by students and their families. The number of student enrollments affect institutional incomes and expenditures. The cost of tuitions and fees determine the students' financial needs which, in turn, influence the financial aid program expenditures and impacts. Thus, student financing and institutional financing are so interrelated that no financial aid bibliography would be complete without including the literature on this subject.

Two issues basic to the discussion of student and institutional financing are: who should pay for the costs of education and how should these payments best be made.

Most observers agree that the costs of education should be apportioned among students and their families, the state and federal governments (through taxation of the general public), and the private sector of the economy (through donations and purchase of services). They also agree that the amount contributed by each of these groups should somehow be related to the benefits it receives.

The question of who should pay the costs of education is discussed by the Carnegie Commission on Higher Education (1973) in a widely publicized report which makes recommendations on the financing of higher education. Another widely read report on financing higher education was put out by the Committee for Economic Development (1973). Bowen (1974) presents a helpful comparison of these and other reports by national study groups. Bowen and Servelle (1972) discuss the difficulties of using the benefit theory to decide who should pay for education. Byrnes (1971) and Millett (1972) also present position papers on this issue.

Two collections of papers on the economics and financing of education provide helpful overviews of student and institutional financing (College Entrance Examination Board, 1967; Hewitt, 1972). Mills (1972) and Shulman (1971) supply useful, but now somewhat dated, bibliographies on the topic.

An early report of a federal task force describes the financial condition of institutions and students in the late 1960s. The report summarizes national policy issues and offers data related to those issues (U.S. Department of Health, Education, and Welfare, 1969). A more comprehensive study is provided by the federally sponsored National Commission on Financing of Postsecondary Education (1973). The commission's voluminous report describes the structure of institutional and student financing and makes a series of recommendations concerning the funding of both. Shaw (1974) discusses the commission's major recommendations.

Although most observers believe that governments should pay some portion of the costs of education, they disagree on the most efficient and effective method of government subsidization. Some parties favor direct subsidies to institutions, thus keeping tuitions and costs to students at a minimum and reducing the overall need for financial aid. Others believe that student fees should more closely approximate the true costs of education, and that needy students should receive direct aid to meet those higher costs. Those who favor this latter approach believe it would create a free market in which public and private institutions could compete equally. Public institutions are currently able to charge lower tuitions because of direct governmental appropriations. Were it not for these appropriations, public and private tuitions would be comparable and students receiving direct financial aid would have greater freedom to choose among public and private institutions. The strengths and weaknesses of this free-market concept are discussed by Leslie and Johnson (1974) and Levin (1973).

Those who favor direct subsidies to students also believe that the present system of governmental appropriations to institutions discriminates against low-income families and their children. These observers argue that (1) the tax structure, which supports governmental appropriations, requires low-income families to pay proportionately more for the educational services they receive, and (2) tuition subsidies to public colleges represent a kind of "hidden financial aid" for affluent students. In other words, tuition subsidies reduce costs to high-income students who could reasonably afford to pay them, and thus represent an inefficient and inequitable use of governmental funds.

A discussion of these viewpoints is offered by Windham (1972a). Two items published early in the decade discuss the issue from contrasting viewpoints (Roose, 1970; Thackrey, 1971). Other discussions on this issue are presented by Ford (1972), Maltby (1973), Weathersby (1976), and Young (1970). Thompson and Hearn (1971) report that student aid ranked first among federal funding techniques favored by presidents of private colleges.

The Federal Higher Education Amendments Act of 1972 provided for aid of both types: direct aid to students through the Basic Educational Opportunity Grant Program and aid to institutions through cost-of-education grants based on enrollment of needy students. The latter program has not yet been funded or implemented. Mallan (1975) discusses the cost-of-education legislation and the controversy surrounding it. The impact of the BEOG program on the financing of community colleges is discussed by Leslie, et al. (1975) and Ebersole (1973).

One plan for financing postsecondary education that has received considerable attention in the literature involves pricing it at full cost and using governmental resources to support long-term, income-contingent loans to students. Windham (1972b) describes how full-cost tuition pricing structures and long-term loans could be used to achieve equity and efficiency in financing students and colleges. Because of new questions about higher education finance, Windham (1974) further proposes a total reassessment of the assumptions on which need analysis is based.

Barnes, et al. (1972) report on a study that used a simulation model to demonstrate that subsidies to students rather than institutions would produce a more equitable financing system. In their plan, education would be priced at or close to full cost, students from families with poverty-level income would receive some grant assistance and some loan assistance, and all other students would have access to long-term, income-contingent loans to help meet their educational costs.

A plan for the State of Ohio in which education is priced at or close to full cost and paid for by students through income-contingent loans is discussed in two items (Curran, 1972; Raymond and Sesnowitz, 1976). A new proposal for financing postsecondary education in New Jersey through increased aid to students and reduced institutional subsidies is discussed by Braun (1976) and by the New Jersey Commission on Financing Postsecondary Education (1976).

Four present positions on full-costing, loan-financed education (Alchian and Allen, 1968; Collins, 1970; Mallan, 1973; Morrell, 1972). Berner, et al. (1972) recommend that income-contingent loans be applied on a small scale, rather than a nationwide basis.

Zacharias (1969) presents one of the earlier, more widely discussed plans for educational financing through student loans. Additional discussions of the role of loan plans in financing education are offered by Bowen (1969), Hartman (1971), Ostar (1976), and Wright (1974).

Tuition costs and tuition policies in general have received considerable attention in the literature of financial aid. O'Neill (1973) provides statistical data on the relationships of tuitions to instructional costs, financial aid, and cost-price indexes. Data from several sources are analyzed to show how tuitions create access barriers to students in a study by the American Association of State Colleges and Universities (1976). A collection of papers on low-tuition policy provides an excellent overview of the issues of this topic (Young, 1974). Mallan (1976) examines various viewpoints regarding low tuitions.

Analyses by Graziano (1972) and Johnson and Leslie (1976) indicate that increasing tuitions will produce negative results, especially for middle-income students. Winter (1972) analyzes the potential effects of tuition increases on students from various income levels.

Burns and Cheswick (1970) and Kimball (1974) discuss graduated tuition plans based on student ability to pay and Carbone (1973) describes the potential effects of several different tuition systems. Simon (1974) and Richardson (1974) discuss tuition policies for community colleges.

Millett (1974a) believes that the tuition gaps between public and private institutions should be reduced by direct subsidies to private institutions rather than students, on the basis of the number of state residents enrolled.

A major impetus for the widespread discussion of who should pay for postsecondary education was generated by the financial plight of many postsecondary institutions in the late 1960s and early 1970s. This situation is reviewed in three studies (Byrne and Tussing, 1971; Cheit, 1971; Jellema, 1973). Congressman Brademas (1971) discusses the financial crisis of students and institutions and Bowen (1975) describes the effects of economic inflation and recession on higher education in general.

Much of the literature agrees that the federal government should act to alleviate the financial crisis and several documents offer proposals for action. Froomkin (1970) describes the potential costs of federal action in support of students and institutions. Later analyses of various proposals are offered by Mathematica, Inc. (1971), Leslie (1972), Johnstone (1972), and Hartman (1972, 1974). Muirhead (1973) describes five different forms of federal assistance to students and their relationship to educational finance. Senator Muskie (1972) offers some proposals to solve the financial plight of higher education. Weldon and Makowski (1976) report on the current distribution of federal funds among institutions in the West.

The actions of state governments in support of postsecondary education are examined in several documents. Millett (1974b) discusses the use of budgetary formulas in state allocations to institutions. The Academy for Educational Development (1973) reports on a study of the structure of education finance in California. McGuire (1976) refutes the argument that the funding of California public higher education discriminates against students from lower-income families. Another Academy for Educational Development (1972) study reviews the financing structure of postsecondary education in Oregon, offering several alternative financial structures and systems. A later study of Oregon's subsidies to higher education suggests that portable grants to students would produce more efficient and equitable financial support of postsecondary education (Wish and de Vriend, 1973).

Finally, two additional plans to help finance higher education are discussed. Leslie (1976) supports the use of a higher education tax allowance to help students and parents pay for education. O'Hearne (1972) believes that awarding needy talented students advanced placement credit will help to ease the financial burdens of students and institutions.

VI.1. Academy for Educational Development. *Financing postsecondary education in California.* Palo Alto, Calif.: Academy for Educational Development, 1973.

Report on the structure of educational finance in the state. Concludes that increased funding is necessary to meet demands of increased enrollments; cost-benefit analysis is of limited utility in determining who should pay for education; tuition charges and student aid represent major pricing variables; loans based on future income represent an attractive means of providing aid to students; the state must decide among financing options that direct money to students, institutions, or both.

VI.2. Academy for Educational Development. *Financing postsecondary education in Washington, A report to the council on higher education, State of Washington.* Palo Alto, Calif.: Academy for Educational Development, 1972.

Reviews the financing of postsecondary education in the state, emphasizing the need for users of higher education and the state to share the costs. Offers several alternative financial structures and systems.

VI.3. Alchian, A. A. and Allen, W. R. What price zero tuition? *The Michigan Quarterly Review,* Vol. 7, Fall 1968, pp. 269–272.

Believes that zero-tuition plans provide the talented with a subsidy to exploit this advantage. Favors a tuition system supported by income-contingent loans.

VI.4. American Association of State Colleges and Universities. *Basic facts about tuition and educational opportunity.* Low Tuition Fact Book No. 8. Washington, D.C.: American Association of State Colleges and Universities, 1976.

Analyzes data from several sources to show that tuition charges create a barrier to access to postsecondary education.

VI.5. Barnes, G. W., Erickson, E. W., Hill, W., and Winokur, H. S. *Direct aid to students: A radical structural reform.* Washington, D.C.: ICF, Inc., 1972.

Using a simulation model, and data from a sample of 1970 North Carolina high school seniors, this study analyzes the effects of changes in costs on college attendance by family income, race, high school achievement, and family size. It then examines the effects of direct student aid versus institutional aid and concludes that subsidies linked to the enrollment of needy students would result in a more effective and efficient means of financing postsecondary education.

VI.6. Beck, N. E. The financing of American higher education. *Financial Aid Report,* Vol. 1, September 1971.

Briefly describes the different philosophies of financing higher education and their relationship to federal legislation before Congress. Believes that aid administrators should voice their opinions in the debates on behalf of students.

VI.7. Berner, R., et al. *A new variant of the Educational Opportunity Bank designed for stability and ease of administration in "small-scale" application.* Philadelphia, Pa.: Pennsylvania University, 1972.

Describes variations on the Educational Opportunity Bank: semi-conventional, full-contingent, and partially contingent loan plans. Discusses the economic theory of the ideal contingent loan repayment program.

VI.8. Bowen, H. R. Financing higher education: The current state of the debate. *Liberal Education,* Vol. 60, March 1974, pp. 45–60.

Examines six major reports by eminent national groups on the financing of higher education: the Carnegie Commission on Higher Education, the Committee for Economic Development, the National Board on Graduate Education, the National Commission on the Financing of Postsecondary Education, the National Council of Independent Colleges and Universities, and the Special Task Force to the Secretary of the Department of Health, Education, and Welfare.

VI.9. Bowen, H. R. Tuitions and student loans in the finance of higher education. In *The economics and financing of higher education in the United States.* Washington, D.C.: Government Printing Office, 1969a.

Proposes that students be financed partly by grants based on the difference between a minimum college budget and their financial capability; that students receive loans to take care of costs not covered by grants; and, that the federal government give unrestricted grants to institutions as institutional costs increase.

VI.10. Bowen, H. R. Who pays the higher education bill? In *Proceedings of a symposium on financing higher education.* Atlanta: Southern Regional Education Board, 1969b.

Discusses the sources of financial support to students and institutions. Offers a proposal for direct financial aid to students rather than institutions.

VI.11. Bowen, H. G. and Servelle, P. *Who benefits from higher education – and who should pay?* Washington, D.C.: American Association for Higher Education, 1972.

Because both students and society benefit from higher education, the authors argue that its costs should be divided between the two by sound economic theory.

Benefit theory can be used to determine how much should be paid but the difficulty is in choosing which version of the theory to use – one based on justice, or one based on efficiency and marginal analysis.

VI.12. Bowen, W. G. The effects of inflation/recession on higher education. *Educational Record,* Vol. 56, Summer 1975, pp. 149–155.

Proposes a national program of competitive fellowship awards designed to help solve the financial problems of public and private colleges.

VI.13. Brademas, J. The financial crisis in American higher education. *Journal of Student Financial Aid,* Vol. 1, May 1971, pp. 26–52.

A congressman's observations on the financial plight of students and institutions and some potential solutions to those problems.

VI.14. Braun, R. J. New Jersey's free market plan. *Change,* Vol. 8, August 1976, pp. 18–21.

Discusses New Jersey's new free market fiscal plan which calls for the reduction of institutional subsidies and an increase in direct aid to students.

VI.15. Bureau of Research in Higher and Professional Education. *The "voucher system" and higher education in New York state.* Albany, N.Y.: New York State Department of Education, 1970.

Discusses the advantages and disadvantages of a voucher system in support of postsecondary students and institutions in New York. Reviews several alternative plans.

VI.16. Burns, J. M. and Chiswick, B. R. Analysis of the effects of a graduated tuition program at state universities. *Journal of Human Resources,* Vol. 5, Spring 1970, pp. 237–245.

Discusses the effects of a tuition program that increases charges according to a student's ability to pay. Predicts that there would be a decrease in the average wealth of students' families and an increase in average quality of students. It would also result in a decrease in the state support required for public colleges.

VI.17. Byrnes, J. C. On the growth and financing of postsecondary education: Who pays, student or taxpayer? *Notes on the Future of Education,* Vol. 2, Summer 1971, pp. 5–9.

Describes the financial crisis in higher education. Proposes two programs to alleviate the crisis: (1) a general per student-year grant sufficient to provide a basic level of resources to educational institutions and (2) a program to permit students to finance educational expenses through a government postsecondary education tax foundation.

VI.18. Byrnes, J. C. and Tussing, A. D. *The financial crisis in higher education: Past, present, and future.* Syracuse, N.Y.: Syracuse University Research Corporation, 1971.

Reviews the history of postsecondary education financing. Suggests that the federal government adopt a program that combines aid to institutions and to students.

VI. 19. Carbone, R. F. The future of the low-tuition system. *Educational Record,* Vol. 54, Fall 1973, pp. 265–270.

Discusses institutional practices that threaten the low-tuition system. Believes that alternative tuition systems should be developed to enhance student access to colleges across the nation as well as in their own states. Outlines criteria for analysis of new tuition plans.

VI. 20. Carlson, D. E. *Access and choice in higher education: Alternative measures and implications for planning.* Davis, Calif.: University of California, Department of Agricultural Economics, 1976.

Discusses access measures and their utility in policy planning from the viewpoint of institutional supply of and student demand for education.

VI. 21. Carnegie Commission on Higher Education. *Higher education: Who pays? Who benefits? Who should pay?* New York: McGraw-Hill, 1973.

After reviewing aggregated data from a variety of sources, the commission makes 13 recommendations regarding the pricing and financing of higher education. Some of the recommendations are controversial: By 1980 the federal government should pay for half the governmental support of higher education. Colleges should charge differential tuition rates for underclassmen, upperclassmen, and graduate students. States should take steps to narrow tuition differentials between public and private education. Public college tuitions should be permitted to gradually rise to one-third educational costs.

VI. 22. Carnegie Commission on Higher Education. *Tuition: A supplemental statement to the report of the Carnegie Commission on Higher Education on "Higher education: Who pays? Who benefits? Who should pay?"* Berkeley, Calif.: Carnegie Commission on Higher Education, 1974.

Presents supplemental information to the initial Carnegie Commission report on tuition (See preceding item). Compares commission recommendations with those of other public and private agencies.

VI. 23. Cheit, E. F. *The new depression in higher education: A study of financial conditions at 41 colleges and universities.* New York: McGraw-Hill, 1971.

Case studies of the financial situations at 41 colleges based on interviews and examination of institutional financial records. Finds that seven out of ten are in financial trouble or soon will be.

VI. 24. College Entrance Examination Board. *The economics of higher education.* New York: College Entrance Examination Board, 1967.

Collection of papers on the structure, operation, and management of the economics and financing of postsecondary education.

VI. 25. Collins, C. C. Financing higher education: A proposal. *Educational Record,* Vol. 51, Fall 1970, pp. 386–377.

Proposes a revolving federal fund to cover operating costs of public and private institutions. A federal agency would be set up to authorize loans covering operating costs for students while they attend college. Repayments would be based, in part, on the student's postcollege employment earnings.

VI.26. Committee for Economic Development. *The management and financing of colleges.* New York: Research and Policy Committee, Committee for Economic Development, 1973.

Discusses the national goals of higher education, the structure of higher education management responsibility and authority, the relationships between management and educational policy, and a strategy for better targeted and increased financial support of higher education. Recommends that tuitions be increased to meet 50 percent of instructional costs, that governments increase aid to needy students to meet those costs, and that governments continue general-purpose grants and appropriations to institutions.

VI.27. Consumer Rights Research Center. *Issues of grants and loans to individuals, Oregon as a case study. An interim report.* Eugene, Ore.: Consumer Rights Research Center, Oregon University, 1971.

Analyzes the current system of financing higher education in Oregon and proposes a voucher-system alternative.

VI.28. Curran, D. G. The Ohio plan for financing higher education. *Intellect,* Vol. 101, October 1972, pp. 31-33.

Describes the advantages of a plan by which public college students repay tuition costs after college.

VI.29. Ebersole, J. F. *The interim effect of federal student aid policy on the community college financial aid officer through Basic Educational Opportunity Grants.* Fort Lauderdale, Fla.: Center for Professional Development, Nova University, 1973.

Examines the impact of federal student aid policies on institutional funding and the autonomy of community colleges.

VI.30. Ford, L. C. Institutional aid. *Journal of Law and Education,* Vol. 1, October 1972, pp. 541-586.

Explains why various public and private agencies are calling for general aid to postsecondary institutions as well as increased aid to students.

VI.31. Froomkin, J. *Aspirations, enrollments, and resources: The challenge to higher education in the seventies.* Washington, D.C.: U.S. Department of Health, Education, and Welfare, 1970.

Estimates the federal resources that would be required by 1976 to support postsecondary students and institutions. Considers two levels of support—minimal and that which would achieve equality of opportunity for low-income students.

VI.32. Funk, H. J. Price elasticity of demand for education at a private university. *Journal of Educational Research,* Vol. 66, November 1972, pp. 130–134.

Seeks to determine the coefficient of price elasticity for the demand for education at the undergraduate level for a private university.

VI.33. Graziano, A. F. *Some factors being overlooked as we increase tuition at our public senior institutions.* Champaign, Ill.: University of Illinois, 1972.

Believes that tuition increases will lead to spiralling increases in the future; to neglect of qualitative consideration of applicants when choosing a college; to neglect of the price elasticity of the demands for education; to negative effects on middle-income families not eligible for aid; and to the lowering of nonresident tuitions by some institutions in order to fill their facilities.

VI.34. Hartman, R. W. *Credit for college: Public policy for student loans.* New York: McGraw-Hill, 1971.

Examines past and present public policy regarding student loans and the wide range of positions taken on the use of loans to finance students and higher education.

VI.35. Hartman, R. W. *Financing the opportunity to enter the "educated labor market."* General Series Reprint No. 285. Washington, D.C.: The Brookings Institution, 1974.

Describes alternative patterns of financing higher education in the 1970s and how these patterns may affect the characteristics and supply of educated labor.

VI.36. Hartman, R. W. *Higher education subsidies: An analysis of selected programs in current legislation.* Washington, D.C.: The Brookings Institution, 1972.

A quantitative and qualitative analysis of various proposals for subsidizing higher education.

VI.37. Haywood, W. T. *Student financial aid: True costs.* NACUBO Professional File, Vol. 8, No. 4. Washington, D.C.: National Association of College and University Business Officers, 1976.

Examines the hidden costs of student financial aid in institutional budgets, noting that there has been a correlation between annual institutional deficits and appropriations for student aid. Discusses implications of aid program regulations for institutions and students.

VI.38. Hewitt, R. G. (Ed.) *Public policy for the financing of higher education.* Wellesley, Mass.: New England Board of Higher Education, 1972.

A collection of 16 papers on the financing of higher education. Topics include: the forms of public financing of higher education; public responsibility for financing private institutions; and the educational, economic, and political conditions surrounding financial aid and policy decisions.

VI.39. Jefferson, J. and Moulton, W. H. Paying for college with student life insurance. *College Board Review,* No. 93, Fall 1974, p. 18.

Proposes a federal national life insurance program to support college costs of financially needy students. The federal government would collect premiums on the policy through the IRS, pay colleges for the students' costs of attendance, and receive reimbursements of its expenses as the sole beneficiary of the policy.

VI.40. Jellema, W. W. *From red to black?* San Francisco: Josey-Bass, Inc., Publishers, 1973.

Documents the fiscal health of 554 private four-year colleges, reporting on where resources come from, how expenditures are made, and the consequences of deficit spending. Describes the role of direct and indirect student aid in institutional finance.

VI.41. Johnson, G. P. and Leslie, L. L. Increasing public tuition in higher education: An alternative approach to the equity issue. *Educational Administration Quarterly*, Vol. 12, Winter 1976, pp. 27–42.

Analyzes the potential impact of increased public college tuition, viewing tuitions as a form of taxation. Concludes that middle-income families would bear disproportionate burdens after tuition increases.

VI.42. Johnstone, D. B. Federal support for higher education. *Financial Aid Report*, Vol. 2, November 1972.

Analyzes the financial plight of colleges, especially private institutions, and suggests positive directions for federal support.

VI.43. Kimball, J. Alternative to student financial aid. *Financial Aid Report*, Vol. 3, January 1974.

Believes that state and federal subsidies should provide a financial floor to institutions and that students should be charged tuitions based on their ability to pay the costs from current and future income.

VI.44. Lantz, B. G., Jr. Financial aid and the future of private colleges. *Liberal Education*, Vol. 61, October 1975, pp. 385–398.

Suggests that private colleges deal with financial aid problems by "competing" in programs, not in cash incentives to students.

VI.45. Leslie, L. L. Higher education tax allowances: An analysis. *Journal of Higher Education*, Vol. 47, September 1976, pp. 497–522.

Discusses potential forms of tax allowances and specific bills and proposals now being considered. Concerned with tax deductions, tax credits, amortized tax credits, and tax deduction/credit options.

VI.46. Leslie, L. L. *The rationale for various plans for funding American higher education.* University Park, Pa.: Center for the Study of Higher Education, Pennsylvania State University, 1972.

Discusses various methods for the funding of higher education. Takes the position that society, and not the individual, must bear the major portion of educational costs.

VI.47. Leslie, L. L. and Johnson, G. P. The market model and higher education. *Journal of Higher Education,* Vol. 45, January 1974, pp. 1–20.

Discusses the trend toward governmental support of higher education through direct aid to students. Identifies several weaknesses in the rationales behind this trend.

VI.48. Leslie, L. L., et al. Financing postsecondary education through students: Windfall profit or recession for community colleges? *Community College Review,* Vol. 2, March 1975, pp. 14–34.

Discusses the potential effects on community colleges of government attempts to channel aid through students. Data from five states indicate that such programs will prove detrimental to the finances of community colleges.

VI.49. Levin, H. M. Vouchers and social equity. *Change,* Vol. 5, October 1973, pp. 29–33.

Believes that vouchers for higher education may somewhat increase efficiency and equity in institutional operations but that overall effects will not be changed because of uneven governmental financing.

VI.50. Mallan, J. P. Educational finance and student loans. *Community and Junior College Journal,* Vol. 43, December–January 1973, pp. 12–13.

Lists new developments in student loans and educational finance that affect community colleges.

VI.51. Mallan, J. P. The case for low tuition. *Change,* Vol. 8, September 1976, pp. 48–49.

Examines the case for low tuition from various viewpoints.

VI.52. Mallan, J. P. The cost-of-education controversy. *Change,* Vol. 7, June 1975, p. 44.

Discusses federal program to provide direct institutional aid to public and private colleges on the basis of the number of enrollees receiving federal student aid.

VI.53. Maltby, G. P. Aid to individuals versus aid to institutions: A discussion of basic issues. *Notre Dame Journal of Education,* Vol. 4, Fall 1973, pp. 258–267.

Examines issue of direct financial aid to individuals and means of allocating public money for postsecondary education.

VI.54. Mathematica, Inc. *An economic analysis of alternative programs to finance higher education.* Bethesda, Md.: Mathematica, Inc., 1971.

Examines the economic and budgetary implications of federal aid to students and discusses potential consequences of alternative approaches to student access and financing of higher education.

VI.55. Mathematica, Inc. *Enrollment and financial aid models for higher education, Phase II, Final report.* Bethesda, Md.: Mathematica, Inc., 1971.

Reports on four models used to forecast enrollment and financial needs of students in postsecondary education. Utilizes data from several national surveys to compute total financial needs and to estimate the costs of alternative federal aid programs.

VI.56. McClure, P. Grubstake: A radical proposal. *Change,* Vol. 8, June 1976, pp. 38–44.

Proposes that each citizen receive $10,000 on the individual's 18th birthday. The money could be drawn through increased salary or used for further education or financial investments.

VI.57. McGuire, J. W. The distribution of subsidy to students in California public higher education. *Journal of Human Resources,* Vol. 11, Summer 1976, pp. 343–353.

Presents two arguments against an earlier study indicating that subsidies in California public higher education discriminate against students from lower-income families.

VI.58. Millett, J. D. *The budget formula as the basis for state appropriations in support of higher education.* Washington, D.C.: Academy for Educational Development, 1974b.

Discusses use of a formula approach in the preparation and recommendation of state appropriations to public higher education.

VI.59. Millett, J. D. Narrowing the gap in changes between public and private institutions. *Liberal Education,* Vol. 60, March 1974a (Supplement), pp. 156–166.

Discusses the reasons for higher tuitions at private colleges and their implication for student access and institutional finance. Proposes that state governments provide a subsidy to private colleges for each full-time undergraduate resident of the state. The subsidy would equal one-half the average subsidy to public college students.

VI.60. Millett, J. D. Who should pay? *Journal of Higher Education,* Vol. 3, October 1972, pp. 509–516.

Argues that students and society should share the costs of education. The author describes four directions he believes state policy will follow: low-tuition policies will be restricted to two-year colleges; charges at four-year colleges will increase to meet about two-thirds to three-fourths of instructional costs; increasing attention will be given to aiding low-income students; graduate charges will be fixed at 25 percent more than those to undergraduates.

VI.61. Mills, G. H. (Ed.) *Who should pay for postsecondary education?* Denver, Colo.: Education Commission of the States, 1972. (Bibliography)

Bibliography of references on the topic.

VI.62. Morrell, L. R. Full costing approach. *College and University Journal,* Vol. 11, November 1972, p. 45.

Discusses a plan whereby parents or students who are able to do so would pay the full costs of postsecondary education.

VI.63. Muirhead, P. P. Federal aid for postsecondary education. *American Education,* Vol. 9, August–September 1973, pp. 4–8.

Briefly describes five different forms of federal student assistance and their roles in the history of educational finance.

VI.64. Muskie, E. S. United States presidential candidate's views on education: A program for education. *Journal of Continuing Education and Training,* Vol. 1, May 1972, pp. 233–237.

Proposes federal programs to ease the financial plight of higher education.

VI.65. National Commission on the Financing of Postsecondary Education. *Financing postsecondary education in the United States.* Washington, D.C.: Government Printing Office, 1973.

Final report and recommendations of the commission. Analyzes the role of postsecondary education, its national objectives, and current and future financing patterns. Offers recommendations on the assessment of the achievement of national objectives, financial distress among institutions, frameworks for analyzing national policies for financing education, and national standard procedures for cost data collection and reporting.

VI.66. New Jersey Commission on Financing Postsecondary Education. *An analysis of the monetary benefits and costs of higher education in New Jersey in 1975–76.* Princeton, N.J.: New Jersey Commission on Financing Postsecondary Education, 1976.

Study to determine who benefits from higher education in the state and who pays for it. Focuses on the equitability of current state programs and policies in support of students and institutions.

VI.67. O'Hearne, J. J. New college scholarships—Rewards in the coin of the realm. *College Board Review,* No. 83, Spring 1972, pp. 22–24.

Believes that linking academic and financial aid policies by granting advanced placement to talented, needy students will help to relieve the financial plight of colleges and students from middle-income families.

VI.68. O'Neill, J. *Sources of funds to colleges and universities.* Berkeley, Calif.: The Carnegie Commission on Higher Education, 1973.

Statistical analysis on the sources of funds to colleges and universities up to 1967–68. Special emphasis is placed on students as a source of revenue through receipt of tuition and federal financial aid subsidies. Compares trends in instructional costs, financial aid, tuitions, and cost-price indexes.

VI.69. Ostar, A. W. Reply with rejoinder (to Student loans and higher education: A way out). *Intellect,* Vol. 104, April 1976, pp. 480–481.

Does not believe that the proposed College Student Acceptance Corporation, which would make loans to middle-income families, would be an effective means of increasing student access to college.

VI.70. Parr, J. G. A little less of the "Who pays?" . . . A little more of the "What for?" *Canadian Journal of Higher Education,* Vol. 3, 1974, pp. 141–150.

Maintains that funding of postsecondary institutions in Canada should be through student fees with substantial financial aid to promote equal access, to effect a separation between governments and institutions, and to provide greater student choice.

VI.71. Raymond, R. and Sesnozitz, M. The Ohio Plan revisited: Some positive aspects of income contingent loan financing of higher education. *Journal of Student Financial Aid,* Vol. 6, May 1976, pp. 34–44.

Discusses the Ohio Plan for financing higher education which proposes that state subsidies to institutions be converted into interest-free student loans to be repaid on an income-contingent basis.

VI.72. Richardson, R. C., Jr. Tuition in community colleges: Another view. *Community and Junior College Journal,* Vol. 44, June 1974, p. 21.

Believes that tuition charges are acceptable under some conditions if they are accompanied by financial aid programs to ensure equal access.

VI.73. Roose, K. D. Aid to students or to institutions. *Educational Record,* Vol. 51, Fall 1970, pp. 356–67.

Using the criteria of economic efficiency, educational opportunity, responsiveness to students, and the preservation of the dual system of higher education, concludes that aid to students is a more fundamentally sound approach than aid to institutions.

VI.74. Shaw, J. S. National policy and the great tuition debate—Does this man have the solution? *College and University Business,* Vol. 56, January 1974, pp. 25–29.

Discusses the six major recommendations of the National Commission on the Financing of Postsecondary Education.

VI.75. Shulman, C. H. *Financing higher education.* Washington, D.C.: ERIC Clearinghouse on Higher Education, 1971. (Bibliography)

A brief review of various proposed solutions to the financial crisis in higher education. Includes an annotated bibliography.

VI.76. Sidar, A. G., Jr. The need for reform in financing higher education. *College Board Review,* No. 84, Summer 1972, pp. 8–10.

Contends that the financial problems of postsecondary students and institutions are the result of poor balance and lack of coordination in federal and state programs.

VI.77. Simonsen, E. Case against tuition in the community colleges. *Community and Junior College Journal,* Vol. 44, June 1974, p. 20.

Outlines various reasons why community colleges should not charge tuition.

VI.78. Thackrey, R. I. *Comments on the Carnegie Commission report: "Higher education: Who benefits? Who pays? Who should pay?"* 1973. (ERIC ED 093229, HE 005672)

Critical analysis of the major observations and recommendations of the Carnegie Commission report.

VI.79. Thackrey, R. I. Reply to "Aid to students or to institutions?" *Educational Record,* Vol. 52, Winter 1971, pp. 23-30.

Proposes a balanced federal program of financial aid to students and institutions.

VI.80. Thompson, H. L. and Hearn, J. J. Student aid ranks first among five federal funding techniques considered by 57 private college presidents. *College and University Journal,* Vol. 10, January 1971, pp. 18-19.

Reports on a 1970 survey of college presidents' opinions on federal funding. After financial aid to students, the presidents favored grants to institutions, categorial aid, and revenue sharing.

VI.81. U.S. Department of Health, Education, and Welfare. *Toward a long-range plan for federal financial support for higher education: A report to the president.* Washington, D.C.: U.S. Department of Health, Education, and Welfare, 1969.

Report of a Special Task Force. Outlines the basic objectives of federal support of higher education and describes the present financial condition of institutions and students. Summarizes national policy issues and includes data related to those issues.

VI.82. Weathersby, G. B. Institutional versus student aid. In *Current issues in higher education: Individualizing the system.* Vermilye, D. E. (Ed.) San Francisco: Josey-Bass, Inc., Publishers, 1976.

Emphasizes efficiency, effectiveness, and equity as criteria for developing a financing system.

VI.83. Weldon, K. and Makowski, D. *Federal funding of postsecondary education in the 13 western states.* Boulder, Colo.: Western Interstate Commission for Higher Education, 1976.

Reports on the distribution of federal funds in the western states. Major problems examined include BEOG, SEOG, CWSP, NDSL, GSLP, Institutional Development, Social Security Student Benefits, Veterans Administration Benefits, and Research and Development.

VI.84. Wentworth, E. The Higher Education Act and beyond. *Change,* Vol. 4, September 1972, p. 10.

Describes the major facets of the Higher Education Act of 1972 and discusses its potential impact on students and colleges.

VI.85. Windham, D. M. Financial aid, need determination, and higher educational finance: Charting the future. *Financial Aid Report,* Vol. 3, January 1974.

Calls for a total review of the assumptions on which need analysis is based in response to new questions about how costs should be divided among society, parents, and students and what form each parties' contribution should take.

VI.86. Windham, D. M. The efficiency/equity quandry and higher education finance. *Review of Educational Research*, Vol. 42, Fall 1972a, pp. 541–560.

Examines alternative means of financing higher education and how they affect equity of opportunity and efficiency of returns on the societal investment. Believes full-cost tuition and long-term loans can achieve maximum equity and efficiency.

VI.87. Windham, D. M. The financing of American higher education: An economist's reply. *Financial Aid Report*, Vol. 1, December 1971.

Questions whether a strong emphasis on student loans actually limits student choice and whether social benefits derived from higher education merit substantial governmental support.

VI.88. Windham, D. M. Tuition, the capital market, and the allocation of subsidies to college students. *The School Review*, Vol. 80, August 1972b, pp. 603–618.

Proposes a tuition/loan program for college students but believes that colleges are peculiarly inadequate vehicles for redistributing income in favor of the poor.

VI.89. Winter, R. *An analysis of the effects of tuition and financial aid policies in the State of Illinois*. Urbana, Ill.: University of Illinois, 1972. (Dissertation)

Using a computer-simulation program and economic theory, analyzes the results of changing tuition and financial aid on enrollments of students from various income intervals and on changes in unmet costs borne by students from different groups.

VI.90. Wish, J. and de Vriend, W. *Efficiency and equity in postsecondary education through portable grants: Oregon as a case study*. Eugene, Ore.: University of Oregon, 1973.

Analyzes the effects of ways in which state and local taxes are spent on higher education. Discusses components of state subsidies, their relative effectiveness, and how shifts in subsidies could produce more efficient and equitable results.

VI.91. Wish, J. R., et al. If private colleges are pricing themselves out of the market, voucher plan could save them. *College and University Business*, Vol. 52, May 1972, pp. 8–14.

Examines the financial plight of private colleges in Oregon. Demonstrates that 90 percent of the decline in proportional enrollment in private versus public colleges is attributable to tuition differentials. Proposes a voucher system to provide students with access to private colleges whose facilities are underutilized.

VI.92. Wright, G. E., Jr. How should we finance medical education? *Health Manpower Policy Discussion Paper Series*, No. A7. Ann Arbor, Mich.: Michigan University, 1974.

Describes current financing of medical education and suggests a new system which would ensure that all able students have financial access to medical school. The system relies on an Economic Opportunity Bank proposal featuring different kinds of loans repaid under different terms.

VI.93. Young, K. E. (Ed.) *Exploring the case for low tuition in public higher education.* Iowa City, Iowa: American College Testing Program, 1974.

Collection of papers presented at an invitational conference to explore the case for low tuitions and possible lines of research in the economic, social, and political consequences of changes in tuition levels.

VI.94. Young, K. E. New federal support to institutions and students: What emphasis? *Liberal Education,* Vol. 56, May 1970, pp. 305–308.

Believes that support of institutions through federal aid is the best method of providing access to all classes of students.

VI.95. Zacharias, J. R. Educational opportunity through student loans: An approach to higher education financing. In *The economics and financing of higher education in the United States: A compendium of papers submitted to the Joint Economic Committee, Congress of the United States.* Washington, D.C.: Government Printing Office, 1969.

Describes a plan for a student loan bank which lends money to be repaid as a proportion of the student's income over 30 to 40 years. Believes such a system would establish a free market in higher education.

VII. Research on Financial Aid

A significant portion of the literature of financial aid consists of statements of positions on different topics. These items, many of which are based on research, are useful in understanding the many issues and aspects of financial aid. But the empirical researcher who is seeking guidance in the design of financial aid research or who wants to employ data others have collected needs to locate other studies on topics which interest him. To facilitate this process, this chapter lists items which contain empirical data and which are, for the most part, descriptions of studies on various topics.

The items are grouped in seven categories: (1) research on student access, choice, retention, attrition, and achievement and aid needs; (2) research on scholarship, grant, and education benefits programs and their impacts; (3) research on loans, loan programs and their effects; (4) research on student employment and work-study programs; (5) research which has been conducted at the statewide level on various topics; (6) research concerning special student groups; and (7) research on tuitions and other student expenses.

VII.A. Student Access, Choice, Retention, Attrition, and Achievement and Aid Needs

Much of the research and data on student aid is concerned with identifying the personal, academic, financial, and other demographic characteristics of postsecondary students to learn more about the costs paid for education and the methods used to pay them.

A few national studies are cited. Haven and Horch (1972) studied the costs and resources of 1969–70 sophomores in different types of institutions, analyzing the data by student sex and racial-ethnic groups. Stevenson (1972) presents a capsule summary of the results of that study.

In a report prepared for the National Commission on the Financing of Postsecondary Education, Engen, et al. (1973) analyze the resources, characteristics, secondary school preparation, and educational satisfaction and aspirations of 11,000 students in postsecondary education in the United States. Maxey, et al. (1976) describe trends in the characteristics of college-bound students between 1970–71 and 1974–75. Students in the more recent years had greater family incomes but they were also more likely to apply for financial aid and to work while in college, primarily to meet increased college costs. A report from the American College Testing Program (1975) presents a national profile of the characteristics of aid applicants in 1974–75. McMahon and Wagner (1973) report on a national survey of student and family patterns of educational finance and on student aspirations and expectations. Pike (1970) describes the results of a national study of student aid needs in Canada.

Because financial aid programs are designed to enhance student access to and choice of postsecondary institutions, attention has been given to the extent to which these goals are accomplished. Munday (1976) analyzes the college choices of aid applicants and nonapplicants and finds little relationship between choice and college costs and family incomes for either group. However, educational development (as measured by test scores) was shown to have a moderate and consistent relationship to the choice of college; students who had higher scores tended to choose colleges that had higher costs.

The effects of college costs, student ability to pay for those costs, and institutional choices (or the demand for higher education) are studied by Miller (1971). Jackson and Weathersby (1975), after reviewing a number of demand studies, conclude that low-tuition structures and the availability of high grant awards stimulate student enrollment but that enrollment increases in response to student aid are relatively low.

Using Project Talent data and probability theory, Raymond (1976) estimates that even the most effective financial aid policies would have a limited effect on equal access because many other barriers and factors inhibit enrollment of low-income students.

Fenske and Boyd (1971) conclude that awards from the Illinois State Scholarship Program affected student choices of postsecondary institutions. About one-fourth of the aid recipients studied indicated that they would have attended a different college if they had not received state aid. Voda (1973) studies financial aid practices at 20 Illinois community colleges and concludes that financial aid made a difference in whether students attended on a full-time or a part-time basis.

It has been hypothesized that one of the factors affecting the demand for education is the type and amount of aid students receive. Schlekat (1968) analyzes the aid awarded to different groups of students and finds that low-income students received less desirable aid packages than did middle-income students; that is, the former received more of their aid in the form of loans and work rather than grants. However, evidence presented by Fields and LeMay (1973) from a study at Oregon State University show no differences in the matriculation rates of students who received different types or amounts of aid. Anderson, et al. (1973) study the effects of aid and other factors on matriculation at another institution and reach similar conclusions.

The amounts that parents contribute to their children's education and the role that contribution plays in student finance are described in several items. Boyd and Fenske (1976), analyzing data covering a seven-year period, find that parents are contributing decreasing percentages of dollars expected from need analysis estimates and that students appear to be making up the differences through increased loans and term-time employment. Bob (1976) shows that female students received greater-than-expected parental contributions and less financial aid than male students from the same families. Hamilton (1974) finds that over 60 percent of the parents of students at the University of Illinois were contributing the full costs of education for their children. Carpenter (1971) states that only nine percent of the parents of the University of Texas students were contributing the full costs of education for their children. Over one-third of the students at Texas received less than $100 per year from their parents.

The effects of financial aid on attrition and retention are the topic of several studies. Five studies find no significant relationship between financial aid or need and retention or persistence in college (Baber and Caple, 1970; Harris, 1976; Russ, 1973; Selby, 1973; Sutton, 1975). The Harris study (1976) indicates that dropouts had *less* financial need than those who remained in school.

Four other studies find a relationship between financial need and aid and persistence. Astin (1975) and Blanchfield (1971) determine that students who rely more on loans are more likely than those who rely on other types of aid to withdraw from postsecondary education. Kinsey (1972) reports that financial aid was very important to the success of minority/poverty students at Michigan State University. Winder (1972) finds that aided students at Austin College had higher persistence rates than nonaided students. Sheddan (1976) presents a model which employs multiple discriminate function analysis to predict which students will be persisters, transfers, or dropouts.

Nearly all the items in this section were published in the 1970s. Readers who are interested in the research findings of earlier years (which tend to corroborate the findings of the later ones) should consult Nash's (1969) review of the literature.

The research findings do not conclusively indicate that financial aid consistently affects student access, choice, or retention. About the most that can be said is that aid helps accomplish these goals in some instances for some students. Further study is needed in which the many variables affecting access, choice, and retention are isolated and accounted for in the research design. Such a study is likely to be costly and time consuming. However, in view of the need to validate the achievement of financial aid programs and to identify the situations in which goals can be achieved, such research should be conducted.

VII.A.1. American College Testing Program. *Profile of financial aid applicants: Applicants for 1976-77 funds, National normative data.* Iowa City, Iowa: American College Testing Program, 1975.

Describes national norms for users of ACT financial need analysis services in 1974-75. Includes income levels, class levels and loads, occupations of main family wage earner, and expected parental contribution by sex, income, and class level.

VII.A.2. Anderson, J. F., et al. Non-matriculation. *National Association of College Admissions Counselors Journal,* Vol. 18, November 1973, pp. 16–20.

Study of 664 prospective students who were accepted for admission but failed to enroll, to determine what they decided to do and why.

VII.A.3. Astin, A. W. *Financial aid and student persistence.* Los Angeles, Calif.: Higher Education Research Institute, 1975.

A study of the relationship between receipt of different types of financial aid and persistence in college. Concludes that students who rely on loans are more likely to drop out than are those who rely on work, education benefits, or grants.

VII.A.4. Baber, B. B., Jr. and Caple, R. B. Educational Opportunity Grant students: Persisters and nonpersisters. *Journal of College Student Personnel,* Vol. 11, March 1970, pp. 115–119.

Analysis of a sample of first-semester students at the University of Missouri in 1966 revealed a higher persistence rate among EOG recipients than non-recipients. However, no means of differentiating between EOG persisters and nonpersisters were found.

VII.A.5. Blanchfield, W. C. *College dropout identification: A case study.* Utica, N.Y.: Utica College, 1971.

Summarizes research on a statistical method of identifying potentially successful and dropout students. Successful students are more likely to have a greater concern for social issues and to have received a higher percentage of grants than unsuccessful students.

VII.A.6. Bob, S. H. *Parents' financial support of their male and female children's postsecondary education.* College Park, Md.: University of Maryland, 1976. (Dissertation)

Using data from 1974-75 applicants to the Kansas Tuition Grant Program, investigates the nature of college attendance patterns and family financial support within families where a male and a female were both attending college. Finds that females received less student financial assistance, greater parental contributions, and more than the expected parental contributions. The opposite was true for males.

VII.A.7. Boyd, J. D. and Fenske, R. H. Financing of a college education: Theory and reality. *Journal of Student Financial Aid,* Vol. 6, November 1976, pp. 13–21.

Data from three surveys of recipients of Illinois State Scholarship Commission grants (in 1967–68, 1970–71, and 1973–74). The study compares the ways students actually finance their education with the expectations of aid administrators. It was found that parents are contributing increasingly smaller percentages of dollars expected from need analysis, that students are making up the difference in loans and term-time employment, and that summer earnings have remained relatively constant over the six-year period.

VII.A.8. Branson, H. R. Financing higher education for poor people: Fact and fiction. *College Board Review,* No. 77, Fall 1970, pp. 5–9.

Uses data from a variety of sources to show that black students need more financial aid, that most affluent black students are already attending colleges, that 250,000 more black students would have to be enrolled in college to represent 10 percent of all students, and that an additional one billion dollars in aid would be needed to gain 10 percent black student enrollment.

VII.A.9. Carlson, D. E. *A flow of funds model for assessing the impact of alternative student aid programs.* Menlo Park, Calif.: Stanford Research Institute, 1975.

Analyzes the distribution of federal student aid funds to students with different characteristics at various types of institutions. Presents a model for analysis of distributional effects of changes in program policies.

VII.A.10. Carpenter, E. A study of needs and activities of financial aid recipients and non-recipients. *Journal of Student Financial Aid,* Vol. 1, November 1971, pp. 8–17.

Examines the differences in financial need, parental contributions, term-time employment, personal characteristics, and attitudes between aid recipients, aid applicants not receiving aid, and nonapplicants at the University of Texas at Austin in winter, 1970–71.

VII.A.11. Engen, T. R. and Crippen, D. L. *A report presented to National Commission on the Financing of Postsecondary Education, 1973.* (ERIC ED 104186, HE 006292)

National survey of 11,000 students. Describes their characteristics, educational interests, fields of study, student aid resources, other financial resources, secondary school preparation and satisfaction with their education.

VII.A.12. Fenske, R. H. and Boyd, J. D. The impact of state financial aid to students on choice of public or private colleges. *College and University,* Vol. 46, Winter 1971, pp. 98–107.

Reports on the results of a 1968 survey of Illinois State Scholarship recipients.

The survey found that 25 percent of the recipients would have attended a different college if they had not received state aid; eighty percent of those who would have shifted would have gone to public rather than private colleges.

VII.A.13. Ferrin, R. I., Jonsen, R. W. and Trimble, C. M. *Access to college for Mexican Americans in the Southwest.* New York: College Entrance Examination Board, 1972.

Describes various indexes of access to college for Chicano students at 153 institutions in 1971. Found that students at four-year colleges received financial aid that met 25 percent of their costs. Over 60 percent of the students attended two-year colleges where only 10 to 15 percent of their costs were met by aid.

VII.A.14. Fields, C. R. Alaskan natives and Caucasians: A comparison of educational aspirations and actual enrollment. *Journal of Student Financial Aid,* Vol. 5, November 1975, pp. 35–45.

Reports on a 1972 survey of high school seniors and a 1973 follow-up survey to determine students' postsecondary plans and the extent to which those plans changed or were achieved. Data are analyzed by student sex, racial-ethnic background, socioeconomic status, and postsecondary educational plans.

VII.A.15. Fields, C. R. and LeMay M. L. Student financial aid: Effects on educational decisions and academic achievement. *Journal of College Student Personnel,* Vol. 14, September 1973, pp. 425–429.

Examines the effects of specific types and amounts of aid on student matriculation rates, attrition rates, and grade-point averages. Found that, at Oregon State University in 1969–70 and 1970–71, neither types or amounts of aid affected matriculation rates. There were no differences in the attrition rates of aid applicants, aid recipients, and nonapplicants. Concludes that financial concerns have a greater effect on decisions to attend college than on decisions to remain in college.

VII.A.16. Hamilton, J. J. M. *Financial resources and expenditures of students at the University of Illinois at Urbana-Champaign.* Urbana, Ill.: University of Illinois, 1974. (Dissertation)

Surveys 546 sophomore and junior students in 1972–73. Finds that over 60 percent of the students' parents were contributing the full cost of education for their children. The relative amounts of aid received were influenced by sex, race, marital status, class level, and family income.

VII.A.17. Hansmeier, K. K. *Undergraduate expenditures and sources of income on the Bloomington campus of Indiana University, 1970–71.* Bloomington, Ind.: Indiana University, 1972. (Dissertation)

Analyzes the expenditures and income sources of 465 full-time undergraduates. Results compared to similar studies in 1940–41 and 1951–52.

VII.A.18. Harris, M. L. *A study of the relationship between financial need and student withdrawal among state-grant recipients enrolled at community colleges in Ohio.* Pittsburgh, Pa.: University of Pittsburgh, 1976. (Dissertation)

Telephone interviews with 116 withdrawals and 120 nonwithdrawals form the basis for this 1975 analysis. Found no significant differences between the two groups in relation to independent/dependent status, number of dependent children, adjusted effective income, and unmet financial need. Students who withdrew demonstrated less financial need than those who did not.

VII.A.19. Harris, S. E. Student aid. In *A statistical portrait of higher education.* New York: McGraw-Hill, 1972.

Presents 42 charts and tables on general trends in student aid. Most data are for years prior to 1967.

VII.A.20. Haven, E. W. and Horch, D. H. *How college students finance their education: A national survey of educational interests, aspirations, and finances of college sophomores in 1969-70.* Princeton, N.J.: College Scholarship Service of the College Entrance Examination Board, 1972.

Study to determine how students and their families finance the costs of postsecondary education. Data analyzed by student sex, racial-ethnic groups, and types of institutions attended.

VII.A.21. Jackson, G. A. and Weathersby, G. B. Individual demand for higher education: A review and analysis of recent empirical studies. *Journal of Higher Education,* Vol. 46, November-December 1975, pp. 623-652.

Describes empirical evidence on the impact of price changes on student demands for higher education. Suggests that low tuition and high grant awards stimulate enrollment but that enrollment response to increased student aid is relatively low.

VII.A.22. Kinsey, M. *Financial assistance as a significant factor in the educational survival of selected black students at Michigan State University.* East Lansing, Mich.: Michigan State University, 1972. (Dissertation)

Survey of 259 minority students in the University's Development Program in 1972. Found that financial aid ranked as most important factor in educational survival; loans were the least desired form of aid; almost all students' families make contributions to their educational costs; working during the school year doesn't interfere with grades.

VII.A.23. Maxey, E. J., et al. *Trends in the academic abilities, background characteristics, and educational and vocational plans of college-bound students: 1970-71 to 1974-75.* ACT Research Report No. 74. Iowa City, Iowa: American College Testing Program, 1976.

Reports on characteristics, abilities, and plans of ten percent of the ACT test takers in each of the years. Found that family incomes increased, but so did student plans to work and to apply for financial aid while in college.

VII.A.24. McMahon, W. W. and Wagnar, A. P. *A study of the college investment decision.* ACT Research Report 59. Iowa City, Iowa: American College Testing Program, 1973.

Initial report on the U.S. Office of Education-ACT college investment decision study. Results of a 1972 survey of 2,693 students and families revealed patterns of family income and assets, sources of funds, student expenditures, and student aspirations, plans, and expectations.

VII.A.25. Miller, L. S. *Demand for higher education in the United States.* Stony Brook Working Papers, No. 34. Stony Brook, N.Y.: Economic Research Bureau, State University of New York, 1971.

Report on the impact of factors relating to demand for higher education.

VII.A.26. Munday, L. A. *Impact of educational development, family income, college costs, and financial aid in student choice and enrollment in college.* ACT Research Report No. 77. Iowa City, Iowa: American College Testing Program, 1976.

Analysis of two data sets—college bound high school seniors in 1971-72 and financial aid applicants who were freshmen in 1972-73—revealed little relationship between costs of college attended and family income for aid applicants and nonapplicants. Average student educational development (as measured by test scores) has a moderate and consistent relation to college costs, both for college-bound students generally and for aid applicants.

VII.A.27. Nash, G. A review of financial aid research. *National Association of College Admissions Counselors Journal,* Vol. 14, June 1969, pp. 20-27.

Reviews research to date in three areas: (1) attendance and persistence, (2) types of aid, and (3) aid for various types of students.

VII.A.28. Pike, R. N. *Who doesn't get to the university and why: A study on accessibility to higher education in Canada.* Ottawa: Association of Universities and Colleges of Canada, 1970.

Analysis of the effects of the Canada Student Loans Plan on students and student access.

VII.A.29. Raymond, R. D. The impact of financial aid upon equality of opportunity in higher education. *Journal of Student Financial Aid,* Vol. 6, November 1976, pp. 39-51.

Uses Project Talent data and probability theory to estimate the impact of increased financial aid on differences in postsecondary participation rates of high-income and low-income students. Analysis indicates that even the most effective financial aid policies would fall short of achieving equal access for both groups.

VII.A.30. Russ, J. E. *Relationship between ability, family income, and amount of financial aid received by students and their persistence in college.* Commerce, Tex.: East Texas State University, 1973. (Dissertation)

Study of 1971-1973 financial aid recipients at Henderson State College (Arkansas). Found that receipt of financial aid was the variable most significantly related to persistence.

VII. A. 31. Schlekat, G. A. Financial aid decisions and socioeconomic class of applicants. *Journal of College Student Personnel,* Vol. 9, May 1968, pp. 146–149.

Article based on analysis of 15,908 PCS filers who were freshmen in 1965–66 at colleges across the nation. Concludes that students from lower socioeconomic classes were more likely to receive aid but those from upper classes were more likely to receive grant aid in their award packages.

VII. A. 32. Selby, J. E. Relationships existing among race, student financial aid, and persistence in college. *Journal of College Student Personnel,* Vol. 14, January 1973, pp. 38–40.

Reports on a 1969 study of students at the University of Missouri. Finds no significant differences in aid awarded by sex or race and no relationship between receipt of aid and persistence in college.

VII. A. 33. Sheddan, M. K. *Prediction of persistence for college students receiving federal financial aid: A multiple discriminate function analysis.* Knoxville, Tenn.: University of Tennessee, 1976. (Dissertation)

Five multiple discriminate function analyses are used to identify variables that predict whether college freshmen receiving aid at a small liberal arts college will be persisters, transfers, or dropouts.

VII. A. 34. Stanford Research Institute. *Federal programs of student aid by state.* Menlo Park, Calif.: Stanford Research Institute, 1974.

Describes state-by-state distribution of federal student aid by programs and institutions.

VII. A. 35. Stevenson, G. College student's income: Where it comes from, where it goes. *Occupational Outlook Quarterly,* Vol. 16, Fall 1972, pp. 21–25.

A brief summary of the national survey published by E. W. Haven and D. G. Horch, *How College Students Finance Their Education.*

VII. A. 36. Strong, S. R. *Who gets financial aid?* Minneapolis, Minn.: Minnesota University, 1975.

Examines records of 1,048 University of Minnesota students to determine differences between aid recipients, aid applicants who did not receive aid, and non-applicants. Special attention is given to socioeconomic statuses and academic potential.

VII. A. 37. Sutton, L. S. *Analysis of withdrawal rates of students receiving financial aid at Central Florida Community College.* Fort Lauderdale, Fla.: Nova University, 1975. (Practicum)

Reports on a study conducted at Central Florida Community College to determine whether students who receive financial aid withdraw from college at the same rate as those not receiving aid. No significant difference in the withdrawal rates of the two groups was found.

VII.A.38. Voda, F. A. *Relation of attendance patterns of financial aid applicants to financial aid practices in selected Illinois junior community colleges.* Columbia, Mo.: University of Missouri, 1973. (Dissertation)

Survey at 20 colleges to determine if full-time, part-time, or no-show/drop attendance patterns are related to financial aid practices. No differences in family contributions for the three groups were found; need varied among groups by colleges. Concludes that aid awarded to students does make a difference in attendance patterns.

VII.A.39. Winder, J. B. *A comparison of certain factors in students with and without financial aid at Austin College.* Denton, Tex.: North Texas State University, 1972. (Dissertation)

Compares characteristics of 200 students. Found that aid recipients spent more time studying, had more frequent conferences with teachers and counselors, and had a higher retention rate.

VII.B. Scholarships, Grants, and Education Benefits

Much of the research on scholarships and grants and their effects concerns the federal Basic Educational Opportunity Grants BEOG Program and the programs of various states.

Gracie (1976) compares BEOG legislation to that of other federal aid programs and demonstrates how each affects students by levels of income and enrollment at different types of institutions. Reeher and Fielder (1976) use models to test the potential effects on students and institutions of revisions in the BEOG Program. Miller (1976) surveyed institutional financial aid administrators to determine the potential effects of BEOG on student access and choice and on institutional policymaking.

Four studies examine state grant programs in California, New Jersey, New York, and Pennsylvania. Two reports showed that state aid enhanced access and choice and provided indirect assistance to private colleges (Fife, 1975a, 1975b). Leslie and Fife (1974) conclude that state grant programs are responsible for the college attendance of nearly half their aid recipients, that their awards result in increased consumption of higher education, and that the grants contribute to the student's ability to attend private colleges. Van De Water (1976) found that New York State's Tuition Assistance Program helped more New Yorkers to attend private colleges in that state. A longitudinal study of students who received Illinois State Scholarship Commission awards showed that these students had greater access and choice, which, in turn, helped private colleges maintain their enrollments (Boyd and Fenske, 1975).

Sparks (1974) discusses the effects of the Illinois State Scholarship

Commission's need analysis and awards policies on students at Eastern Illinois University. Bergen (1970) compares the grade-point averages of matched samples of Kansas State Scholarship recipients and nonrecipients. He found that the former earned higher grades. In another type of study, Meade (1971) compares the origin, purposes, structure, administration, policies, and problems of state scholarship programs in Illinois, Indiana, Michigan and West Virginia. He suggests a basic design for a model state program.

Two studies are concerned with the effects of grant aid at individual colleges. Burnham (1971) finds that Economic Opportunity Grant recipients at the University of Arkansas had high persistence rates. Williamson (1971) reports that combining state and institutional aid to students at Towson State University (Maryland) provided ideal scholarship support to needy applicants.

As noted in Chapter III, there is a trend among some institutions to award scholarships and grants on the basis of merit without consideration of financial need. In a national survey of this practice, Huff (1975) reports that 75 percent of the institutions involved were small private colleges in the Midwest or South. These schools reported that the practice was effective in encouraging enrollment of talented students.

Owen (1968) uses cost-benefit analysis to demonstrate how scholarship programs can be made more effective and efficient and why its use should direct national policy.

Only two items deal with educational benefits. A comprehensive, comparative study of the G.I. Bill, its effects on students and institutions, and its problems is provided by Bowman, et al. (1973). Blesch, et al. (1976) describe how participants in the Michigan scholarship and grant programs use social security benefits to support educational costs.

VII.B.1. Bergen, G. R., et al. Do scholarships affect academic achievement? *Journal of College Student Personnel,* Vol. 11, September 1970, pp. 383–384.

Compares academic performance of matched samples of nonrecipients of aid and State of Kansas Scholarship winners for 1963 through 1965. Found that grant recipients earned higher grade averages.

VII.B.2. Blesch, T., et al. Utilization of social security educational benefits. *Journal of Student Financial Aid,* Vol. 6, 1976, pp. 13–25.

Survey of 1973-74 participants in the Michigan scholarship and grant programs shows that utilization of social security benefits is significantly greater than expected from program assessment procedures.

VII.B.3. Bowman, J. L., Volbert, J. J., and Hahn, J. V. *Educational assistance to veterans: A comparative study of three* G.I. *bills.* Princeton, N.J.: Educational Testing Service, 1973.

Compares the operation of the educational assistance programs available to veterans of World War II and the Korean conflict with programs available to veterans of post-Korean conflicts. Study deals with the quality of the programs, veterans' participation in them, the adequacy of benefits to students, institutions and society, the nature and degree of abuse in the programs, and the execution and administration of the programs.

VII.B.4. Boyd, J. D. and Fenske, R. H. *A longitudinal study of Illinois State Scholarship Commission monetary award recipients, 1967–1974.* Deerfield, Ill.: Illinois State Scholarship Commission, 1975.

Surveys Illinois state scholarship and grant winners in 1967–68, 1970–71, and 1973–74. Discusses opinions and attitudes regarding student aid and the impact of awards on student access, choice, and financing of college costs. How the findings relate to program policies and practices is also discussed.

VII.B.5. Burkhard, E. L. *A study of the Wyoming legislative scholarship.* Greeley, Colo.: University of Northern Colorado, 1970. (Dissertation)

Analyzes the effectiveness of the Wyoming program as a means of recruiting high school graduates to teacher education programs. Concludes that program is not effective.

VII.B.6. Burnham, J. E. *The effectiveness of the Educational Opportunity Grant Program at the University of Arkansas as measured by student persistence.* Fayetteville, Ark.: University of Arkansas, 1971. (Dissertation)

Studies the demographic and intellective characteristics of 348 students who received EOG awards during the 1966–67 to 1969–70 period to ascertain the effectiveness of the program as measured by college persistence.

VII.B.7. Fife, J. D. *The college student grant study.* University Park, Pa.: Center for the Study of Higher Education, The Pennsylvania State University, 1975a.

Examines the validity of the following basic assumptions underlying state grant programs: student aid increases access to postsecondary education; aid enhances student choices; financing higher education through aid to students helps private colleges. Concludes that the assumptions are valid but that further research on the impact of grants is needed.

VII.B.8. Fife, J. D. *The impact of scholarships and grants on students' college decisions.* University Park, Pa.: The Pennsylvania State University, 1975b. (Distation)

Examines the aid program as a mechanism to help achieve equal access and choice and increase the dynamics of the marketplace. Used data from 1972–73 state grant recipients in New York, New Jersey, Pennsylvania, and California. Data are analyzed by students' financial resources, expenses, socioeconomic status, attendance patterns, and perceived impact of state aid. Concludes that programs significantly enhance access and choice.

VII.B.9. Fife, J. D. and Leslie, L. L. The college student grant study: The effectiveness of student grant and scholarship programs in promoting equal educational opportunity. *Research in Higher Education,* Vol. 4, No. 4, 1976, pp. 317–333.

Examines the extent to which state grant programs in California, New Jersey, New York, and Pennsylvania promote student access and choice. Concludes that the programs are responsible for college attendance of nearly half their recipients.

VII.B.10. Gracie, L. W. *An analysis of the federal student financial aid policies as developed in the BEOG program when compared to traditional federal student aid programs.* Tallahasee, Fla.: Florida State University, 1976. (Dissertation)

Compares federal programs in terms of their legislation and, using aggregate data, their outputs to students from different income levels and to different types of institutions.

VII.B.11. Huff, R. P. No-need scholarships: What 859 colleges said about granting money to students without regard to financial need. *College Board Review,* No. 95, Spring 1975, pp. 13–15.

Report on a national survey which found that over half the colleges contacted were making merit awards. Over 75 percent of those making awards were smaller private institutions, typically located in the Midwest and the South. About half these institutions said that their merit awards were effective in achieving their underlying purposes.

VII.B.12. Leslie, L. L. and Fife, J. D. The college student grant study: The enrollment and attendance impacts of student grant and scholarship programs. *Journal of Higher Education,* Vol. 45, December 1974, pp. 651–671.

Reports that state grant and scholarship awards, when considered by students as money income, result in increased consumption of higher education and redistribution of students to private colleges.

VII.B.13. Meade, R. C. *A description of four state competitive scholarship programs of states which have membership in the Mid-West association of student financial aid administrators.* Muncie, Ind.: Ball State University, 1971. (Dissertation)

Describes the competitive scholarship programs of Illinois, Indiana, Michigan, and West Virginia. Compares their origin and purpose, structure and administration, selection processes, and problems. Suggests a basic design for a model state program.

VII.B.14. Miller, D. A. *The perceived effect of BEOG legislation upon student access, student choice, and organization policy-making within four-year degree granting institutions in the state of Ohio.* Oxford, Ohio: Miami University, 1976. (Dissertation)

Surveyed financial aid administrators to answer the questions posed by the title. Found that administrators were critical of the BEOG, saying it did not put choice in the hands of students. Public college administrators favored block grants to institutions; those at private colleges favored direct aid to students and tuition-offset grants.

VII. B. 15. Owen, J. D. *An economic analysis of college scholarship policy.* Baltimore, Md.: Center for the Study of Social Organization of Schools, The Johns Hopkins University, 1968.

Proposes a national scholarship policy based on a cost-benefit analysis of the social value of education. A central college subsidy agency would allocate funds according to the maximum overall contribution of the students. Emphasis would be placed on the present benefits to society, rather than on the students' future economic contributions.

VII. B. 16. Reeher, K. R. and Fielder, E. R. *A critical review and analysis of the federal Basic Educational Opportunity Grants Program and its effect on the Pennsylvania Higher Education Grant Program.* Harrisburg, Pa.: Pennsylvania Higher Education Assistance Agency, 1976.

Reviews the strengths and weaknesses of the BEOG Program and its impact on students and institutions in the state. Then, utilizing a national data file, tests the impact of five alternative revisions to the program on the distribution of aid by income intervals and institutional types.

VII. B. 17. Sparks, S. C. A study of 1973-74 Eastern Illinois University applicants for an award by the Illinois State Scholarship Commission. *Journal of Student Financial Aid,* Vol. 4, November 1974, pp. 13–19.

Results of a study of the financial aid needs and resources and college enrollment of applicants to Eastern Illinois University who were judged to have no need. Found that 80 percent of the applicants enrolled with no aid at all.

VII. B. 18. Van De Water, G. B. *The impacts of New York State's Tuition Assistance Program on the amount and distribution of financial aid resources at highly selective private colleges in New York.* Syracuse, N. Y.: Syracuse University, 1976. (Dissertation)

Uses student survey data to assess the extent to which the TAP was increasing the amount of aid to students and reducing the tuition gap between public and private colleges. Found that aid was increased, more New Yorkers were enrolling, and TAP did not affect the ability-to-pay distribution in the sample population.

VII. B. 19. Williamson, W. W. National survey shows that combining state aid and institutional funds gives ideal scholarship support. *College and University Business,* Vol. 51, November 1971.

Reports on a study at Towson State University (Maryland) which compared that institution's scholarship program to those of other institutions. Concludes that combining state and institutional aid provides ideal scholarship support.

VII.C. Loans and Loan Programs

Several documents in this section concern administrative aspects of loan programs. A report from the American Council on Education (1975) describes the policies, practices, and problems of federal student loan programs. Two studies by the Comptroller General (1974, 1975) of the financial statements of the Student Loan Insurance Fund indicate that records maintained by the fund are inadequate to management needs.

A survey of lenders and borrowers in the federal Guaranteed Student Loan Program (GSLP) indicates that the administrative and loan costs of that program are increasing while lender participation is decreasing (Gordon and Errecart, 1975). One of the factors contributing to decreased lender participation is the high cost of servicing student loans. A study by Technology Management, Inc. (1974) suggests revisions in the program to help reduce servicing costs.

Default rates on student loans also contribute to lower lender participation rates. Pattillo and Wiant (1972) find that borrowers who accept loans late in their academic careers, who had taken previous educational loans, or who came from larger families were likely to have higher-than-average loan repayment delinquency rates. In a study of loan repayment patterns in the National Direct Student Loan Program, Bergen (1972) reports that loan sizes did not affect repayment rates. However, he finds that students with higher grade-point averages were less likely to be delinquent in their loan repayments.

Three studies concern the role of loans in student financing of educational costs. Hartline (1972) finds that student loans play a less significant role than other types of aid or financial resources. Brugel and Hofmann (1974) study the effects of revisions in the Guaranteed Student Loan Program on potential borrowers at Pennsylvania State University in 1973. Their research indicates that the program's needs test requirement substantially withdrew loan resources available to middle-income students. Balderson (1970) believes that one reason students are less likely to accept loans than other forms of aid is that loan repayments are concentrated in earlier years of employment when the net returns from education are concentrated in later years. Students believe that it is less difficult to pay for educational costs from current earnings and other resources than to accept loans. Balderson believes that spreading out loan repayments over longer periods of time and basing them on income-contingencies would make loans more attractive to students.

Johnstone, et al. (1972) report that various income-contingent loan programs would be attractive to potential borrowers at a sample of ten colleges. In spite of the current system of concentrated early repayment plans and other difficulties with aid programs, a national study reveals that 80 percent of the student borrowers had favorable attitudes about educational loans (Harrison, et al., 1972).

Weiss (1970) provides a case study of the effects of a national study of federal student loan programs on policy and policy-makers.

Wedemeyer (1972) provides a review of the literature and research on the federal Guaranteed Student Loan Program and suggests a need for further research on this program and its effects.

VII.C.1. American Council on Education. Federal student loan programs. *Policy Analysis Reports,* Vol. 1, No. 1, 1975.

Discusses the policies, practices and problems of federal student loan programs.

VII.C.2. Balderson, F. E. *The repayment period for loan-financed college education.* Berkeley, Calif.: Ford Foundation Program for Research in University Administration, 1970.

Demonstrates that loan financing of college educational costs in which repayments are concentrated in the earlier years of employment has a deterrent effect on attendance because the net returns from education are concentrated in later years. Advocates extending the loan repayment period and basing repayments on income contingencies.

VII.C.3. Bergen, M. B., et al. Do GPA and loan size affect NDSL repayments? *Journal of College Student Personnel,* Vol. 13, January 1972, pp. 65-67.

A study of 1,374 NDSL borrowers from Kansas State University finds that students with high grade-point averages were less likely to be delinquent in payments and that loan sizes did *not* affect delinquency rates.

VII.C.4. Brugel, J. and Hofmann, G. The revised Guaranteed Student Loan Program: An impact analysis. *Journal of Student Financial Aid,* Vol. 4, March 1974, pp. 11-18.

Assesses the impact of GSLP revisions on potential borrowers at Pennsylvania State University in 1973. Findings suggest that the revisions substantially withdraw the aid previously available to middle-income families. Suggests some program modifications to alleviate this condition.

VII.C.5. Comptroller General of the United States. *Examination of financial statements of Student Loan Insurance Fund, fiscal year 1973.* Washington, D.C.: Government Printing Office, 1974.

Examines the fiscal year 1973 financial statements of the Office of Education's Student Loan Insurance Fund.

VII.C.6. Comptroller General of the United States. *Examination of financial statements of Student Loan Insurance Fund, fiscal year 1974.* Washington, D.C.: Government Printing Office, 1975.

Examines the fiscal year 1974 financial statements of the Office of Education's Student Loan Insurance Fund and discusses problems of the fund. Indicates that records maintained by the Office of Education are inadequate to support financial statements of lenders.

VII.C.7. Gordon, K. F. and Errecart, M. *A survey of lenders in Guaranteed Student Loan Programs.* Bethesda, Md.: Resource Management Corporation, 1975.

National survey of lenders and borrowers in the federal GSLP. Discusses findings in terms of increasing program costs and loan default rates, the extent of future federal liability, and decreasing lender participation in the program.

VII.C.8. Harrison, R. J., et al. Student attitudes toward borrowing and working: Results of national surveys. *College and University,* Vol. 47, Summer 1972, pp. 439–441.

Summarizes the results of two national surveys sponsored by the Office of Education. The surveys revealed that 80 percent of the borrowers had favorable attitudes about borrowing, most frequently when loan administration was good. More than 87 percent of the work-study students were satisfied with their jobs.

VII.C.9. Hartline, J. C. Student financial aid and the role of student loans. *College and University,* Vol. 47, Winter 1972, pp. 106–117.

Using data from diverse sources, found that parental aid, part-time earnings, scholarships, and savings were more frequently used by students to pay educational costs than were loans.

VII.C.10. Johnstone, D. B., Wackman, D. B., and Ward, S. Student attitudes toward income contingent loans. *Journal of Student Financial Aid,* Vol. 2, March 1972, pp. 11–27.

Reports on a survey of student attitudes toward three income-contingent loan plans. Some 430 undergraduate and 507 graduate students at ten colleges were surveyed. Preference among plans was related to expected future income, racial-ethnic group membership, and graduate-undergraduate statuses. The students' current financial statuses were not significantly correlated with references. Discusses results of other studies and their policy implications.

VII.C.11. Pattillo, L. B., Jr. and Wiant, H. V., Jr. Which students do not repay college loans? *Journal of Student Financial Aid,* Vol. 2, May 1972, pp. 32–35.

Study of 408 students who had received a Texas Opportunity Plan Loan in 1966–67 revealed that students who borrowed later in their academic careers, who had had previous loans, or who came from larger families were more likely to be delinquent. Items reflecting financial, rather than biographical, data were better predictors of loan delinquency.

VII.C.12. Technology Management, Inc. *Analysis of student loan special rate allowances and servicing costs.* Cambridge, Mass.: Technology Management, Inc., 1974.

Analyzes the GSLP's special rate allowances and requirements on lender servicing costs. Makes recommendations for improving both aspects of the program. Data include results of a survey of 13 lender and 3 servicing firms.

VII.C.13. Wedemeyer, R. H. A review of the literature and research: Guaranteed Student Loan Program. *Journal of Student Financial Aid,* Vol. 2, November 1972, pp. 32–37.

Reviews research and policy statements contained in 35 documents. Believes there is a great need for further research on GSLP and its impacts.

VII.C.14. Weiss, C. H. *The consequences of the study of federal student loan programs: A case study of the utilization of social research.* New York: Bureau of Applied Social Research, Columbia University, 1970.

Traces the consequences of a study of federal student loan programs on public policymaking.

VII.D. Employment and Work-Study Programs

The primary concern of research items in this area is the effect of employment on academic performance. Several studies show that working at part-time jobs during the school year has no adverse effect on student achievement (Barnes and Keene, 1974; Gaston, 1973; Kaiser and Bergen, 1968).

Augsburger (1974) demonstrates that working students on academic probation did not earn significantly different grades from nonworking students on probation. Deal, et al. (1973) finds that community college students who worked from 14 to 26 hours per week made higher grades than those who worked less or more than this amount. Merritt (1970) believes that working students earn as good or better grades than nonworking students because they are more highly motivated. Kray, et al. (1974) develop an activity index based on hours in employment and coursework. This study indicates that students who spent between 50 and 60 hours per week in class and work earned higher grades than other students.

Friedman, et al. (1973) conduct a national survey of the federal College Work-Study Program, collecting data from students, employers, financial aid administrators, and personnel who administer the program at regional and national levels. Their study describes the characteristics, earnings, types of employment, and job satisfaction of students; the characteristics of institutions and employers; and the ways in which CWSP appropriations are distributed among institutions.

Dugan (1976) reports on a similar study of a large, state-supported work-study program in Washington. The students, institutions, and employers who participated in this program, like those in the federal CWSP, were generally satisfied with it.

Bobrow (1974) analyzes the CWSP operations at a single institution. This study also indicates that work-study students believe they are learning and gaining valuable skills through employment.

Michelotti (1973) reports only a slight increase in the numbers of working students (including work-study students and students who found employment on their own) in the years immediately preceding 1972.

Froomkin (1975) conducts a nationwide survey of the role of student summer and term-time earnings in paying for educational costs. The study identifies a major trend, namely, that students are defraying increasing percentages of their educational costs with earnings. Earnings play an increased role not because students are earning more money, but because, in the more recent years, they are attending lower-cost colleges.

VII. D. 1. Augsburger, J. D. An analysis of academic performance of working and non-working students on academic probation at Northern Illinois University. *Journal of Student Financial Aid,* Vol. 4, June 1974, pp. 30–39.

Examines the differences in academic performance of three groups of students on academic probation: unemployed students, those employed on campus, and those employed off campus. While working students earned higher grade-point averages, the differences were not significant. Findings indicate that students on probation should not be discouraged from working up to 20 hours per week.

VII. D. 2. Barnes, J. D. and Keene, R. A comparison of the initial academic achievement of freshman award winners who work and those who do not work. *Journal of Student Financial Aid,* Vol. 4, November 1974, pp. 25–29.

Compares the academic achievement of financially needy freshmen who worked and those who did not at Southern Illinois University in 1972 and 1973. Findings indicate that part-time work in on-campus jobs does not significantly interfere with academic performance.

VII. D. 3. Bobrow, W. *An examination of the federal college work-study program at Monterey Peninsula College.* Monterey, Calif.: The Monterey Institute of Foreign Studies, 1974. (Thesis)

Survey of students and work-study program supervisors. Data indicate that students believed they were learning and gaining more skills. Supervisors and employers expressed satisfaction with the program.

VII. D. 4. Deal, W. M., Jr., et al. *An analysis of current grade point averages of employed full-time students at Wilkes Community College.* Fort Lauderdale, Fla.: Nova University, 1973. (Practicum)

Analyzes the effects of employment on the grade-point averages of 830 full-time students. Found that students in the College Transfer Program who worked from 14 to 26 hours per week earned higher grades than those who worked over 40 hours per week.

VII.D.5. Dugan, M. *Report on the Washington state work-study program: 1974–75.* Olympia, Wash.: Council for Postsecondary Education, 1976.

A survey of 1974–75 participants in the Washington State College Work-Study Program (WSWSP). Students, employers, and institutions were surveyed. Found that most students were very satisfied with the WSWSP, especially as it gave them practical work experience. Employers liked the WSWSP because it provided a good method of job training for future full-time employees. Institutions were statisfied with the program but suggested a need for money to defray administrative costs and a need for better publicity for the program.

VII.D.6. Friedman, N., Sanders, L. W., and Thompson, J. *The federal College Work-Study Program.* New York: Bureau of Applied Social Research, Columbia University, 1973.

National study based on data obtained from work-study students, employers, financial aid administrators, and personnel administering the program at regional and national levels.

VII.D.7. Froomkin, J. *Trends in sources of student support for postsecondary education.* Special Report No. 16. Iowa City, Iowa: American College Testing Program, 1975.

Study of the impact of student earnings on the total financing of postsecondary education. Concerned with trends in aggregate student earnings; how the earnings increase resources to finance education, raise standards of living, and substitute for parental contributions; the composition of total earnings; and the effects of changing college costs on students' work efforts, earnings, and contributions from assets.

VII.D.8. Gaston, M. A study of the effects of college-imposed work-study programs on grade point averages of selected students at Western Washington State College. *Journal of Student Financial Aid,* Vol. 3, March 1973, pp. 19–26.

Based on data for 1968–69, analysis showed no significant differences in grade-point averages of students who worked up to 15 hours a week and those of nonworking students. Findings further supported the policy of no grade-point average restrictions on receipt of financial aid.

VII.D.9. Kaiser, H. E. and Bergen, G. Shall college freshmen work? *Journal of College Student Personnel,* Vol. 9, November 1968, pp. 384–385.

Study to determine whether working a modest number of hours affects performance of freshmen at Kansas State University. Found that part-time employment had no adverse effect on student grade-point averages.

VII.D.10. Kray, E. J., et al. *The development of an activity index: An analysis of hours worked and credit hours carried by full-time students of Delaware County Community College.* Fort Lauderdale, Fla.: Nova University, 1974. (Practicum)

Uses an activity index to analyze the relationship between work, academic credit hours, and grade-point averages. One hour of academic credit equals 3 activity units; one hour of work equals 1 activity unit. Shows that students with 50 to 59 units earned higher grade-point averages than students with 50 or less.

VII.D.11. Merritt, R. Academic performance of work-study students. *Journal of College Student Personnel,* Vol. 11, May 1970, pp. 173-176.

Compares the performance of relatively affluent members of Greek organizations and that of work-study students. Found no significant difference in their college grade-point averages. Concludes that work-study students are highly motivated.

VII.D.12. Michelotti, K. *Employment of school age youth, October, 1972.* Special Labor Force Report 158. Washington, D.C.: Bureau of Labor Statistics, 1973.

Data on employment of school-age youth shows little change in number of students holding jobs but a large increase among numbers of nonstudents holding jobs.

VII.D.13. Office of Institutional Research. *Follow-up study; Non-academic attrition at Bucks County Community College, 1965-1972.* Newton, Pa.: Bucks County Community College, 1973.

Report on a follow-up study of the educational and employment patterns of students who withdrew from the college. Examines their reasons for withdrawing and their evaluation of college programs and services.

VII.E. Statewide Financial Aid Studies

State student aid program expenditures increased dramatically in the 1970s when the costs of education increased and new groups of low-income students began to attend postsecondary institutions. As a consequence of this growth, and of increased attention to long-range planning for postsecondary education at the state level, states have shown an increased interest in analysis of the students' costs of education, the resources students have and use to meet these costs, and the impact of various student aid programs on student access, choice, and retention. There is also new interest in the administration of state aid programs. Several statewide studies on different aspects of financial aid now appear in the literature. They are described in this section.

Twelve of these studies employed the College Board's Student Resource Survey (SRS) service. The SRS service features a student questionnaire and attendant data processing systems to gather and analyze information on student personal and academic characteristics, their various costs of education, and the types and amounts of financial resources used to defray these costs.

Two statewide SRS studies have been conducted in each of the following states: California (California State Scholarship and Loan Commission, 1972; California State Student Aid Commission, 1976), Pennsylvania (College Entrance Examination Board and Brookdale Associates, 1975a; Pennsylvania Higher Education Assistance Agency, 1975), New Jersey (College Entrance Examination Board and Brookdale Associates, 1975b; New Jersey Commission on Financing Postsecondary Education, 1976), and Washington (Dent, et al., 1972; Donovan, 1977b). SRS studies have also been conducted in Montana (Van Dusen, 1974) and in Oregon (Dent, et al., 1973).

These studies are essentially descriptive in their statistical treatments. They describe patterns of student resources by types of institutions students attend and by students' racial-ethnic groups, dependency statuses, marital statuses, and family incomes. The studies document significant differences in the educational financing patterns of the various groups. They indicate that students need more financial aid than is currently available in order to reasonably afford their educational costs.

One of the New Jersey studies (New Jersey Commission on Financing Postsecondary Education, 1976) is a survey of state residents who were enrolled in postsecondary institutions in another state. This study attempted to determine why state residents left New Jersey for education. A similar SRS study was conducted to determine how students who received grants from the Pennsylvania Higher Education Assistance Agency to attend institutions in other states financed their education and what would happen if their awards could not be used at out-of-state institutions (Van Dusen and Davis, 1975).

The New Jersey Commission on Financing Postsecondary Education (1975) used SRS survey data to conduct a special analysis of the relationships between family financial circumstances and patterns of paying college costs.

Another study methodology, known as aggregate need analysis, has been employed in several statewide studies. This study approach involves surveys of institutions and use of aggregate family income and financial aid data to describe how financial aid and other resources are distributed among students and institutions. Aggregate need analysis was employed in statewide studies in Alabama (Alabama Commission on Higher Education, 1972), Georgia (Creech, 1972), Iowa (Davis and Van Dusen, 1975), Kentucky (College Entrance Examination Board, 1973), and New Jersey (Davis, 1975).

Aggregate need analysis was also used in a study of undergraduates in 14 southern states. The study compared costs, financial aid needs, family resources, and unmet needs of students by family incomes and types of institutions attended (Davis, 1974).

In general, aggregate need analysis studies indicate a need for more student financial aid at most types of institutions. They show that the distribution of financial aid among institutions contributes to a significant proportion of the students' need for more aid. That is, aid is not distributed to institutions in proportion to their students' needs. These studies also show that students from families in the $9,000 to $12,000 income interval generally have greater proportionate needs for more aid than do students from other family income groups. Finally, the studies show that both parents and students make great financial sacrifices to afford the costs of postsecondary education.

Other statewide studies focus attention on the problems of student access and choice in postsecondary education and how financial aid affects these conditions. These include studies in Arkansas (Glover and Chapman, 1975), Delaware (Division of Urban Affairs, 1975), Illinois (Haberaelker and Wagner, 1975), Maryland (Fife, 1975), Montana (Montana State Commissioner of Higher Education, 1976), New York (New York State Board of Regents, 1974), Vermont (Vermont Higher Education Planning Commission, 1976), and West Virginia (West Virginia Board of Regents, 1974).

A study by the Kentucky Higher Education Assistance Agency 1973) identifies all the aid resources available to postsecondary students in that state. Donovan (1977a) documents the increase in aid to students in the State of Washington during the past several years.

Three reports in this section study the administrative effectiveness of aid programs in certain states and offer suggestions for improving and enhancing program effectiveness (Adams, et al., 1974; Arkansas State Department of Higher Education, 1976; Florida State Department of Education, 1976).

The most comprehensive, statewide studies of the administration and coordination of financial aid are those conducted by the California State Student Aid Commission for its master plan for publicly funded financial aid programs (California State Scholarship and Loan Commission, 1975; California State Student Aid Commission, 1977). These planning activities were modeled after those of the National Task Force on Student Aid Problems and address such issues as establishing common aid applications; using common need analysis systems; coordinating aid awards schedules; developing standard student expense budgets; and establishing financial aid data verifications systems, cooperative institutional-state research activities, and cooperative training and development programs for financial aid administrators.

A Virginia atudy is concerned with that state's attempts to support private institutions and their students (Virginia State Council of Higher Education, 1975). Educational Management Services (1973) reports on a series of aid models for Kentucky that are couched in terms of alternative program goals, policies, and practices. The Alabama State Commission on Higher Education (1972) uses aggregate need analysis techniques to estimate the impact of the federal Basic Educational Opportunity Grant Program on student needs in that state.

Two dissertations concern the administration of aid on a statewide basis. Cogdell (1971) analyzes the impact of three federal campus-based aid programs in the District of Columbia, and Erbschole (1976) describes the management, administration, and distribution of financial aid resources at Arizona postsecondary institutions.

Two statewide surveys of the educational and career plans of high school seniors yield data on the impact of financial need and aid on postsecondary planning (College Entrance Examination Board and Brookdale Associates, 1976; Iowa State Higher Education Facilities Commission, 1975).

VII.E.1. Adams, C. F., et al. *Student financial aid in Illinois*. Springfield, Ill.: Illinois Economic and Fiscal Commission, 1974.

Examines the impact and effectiveness of aid programs in Illinois. Part of the analysis is based on a survey of 7,800 public university students. Suggests that a standard application form should be developed, that parents are making considerable sacrifices to meet costs, that small businessmen seem to be treated unfairly in need analysis, and that state programs should develop better means of detecting fraudulent aid applications.

VII.E.2. Alabama Commission on Higher Education. *A study of undergraduate student financial aid in Alabama, 1970-71*. Montgomery, Ala.: Alabama Commission on Higher Education, 1972.

Studies the aggregate costs, student and family resources, financial need, and need for additional aid of undergraduate students at seven types of colleges and universities in the state.

VII.E.3. Alabama State Commission on Higher Education. *A special report: The estimated impact of the Basic Educational Opportunity Grant Program on student financial aid at Alabama colleges and universities, 1972-73*. Montgomery, Ala.: Alabama State Commission on Higher Education, 1972.

Estimates the potential effect of the BEOG on financial aid needs of students at seven types of Alabama colleges. Used data on 1972-73 costs, enrollments, financial needs, and available aid.

VII.E.4. Arkansas State Department of Higher Education. *Confronting student aid problems in Arkansas postsecondary educational institutions.* Little Rock, Ark.: Arkansas State Department of Higher Education, 1976.

Analyzes problems of coordination and administration in student aid in the state. Based, in part, on surveys of student aid directors and high school counselors. Problems included poorly informed students, multiplicity of financial aid forms, lack of adequate student aid funds, and complex federal procedures.

VII.E.5. California State Scholarship and Loan Commission. *Master plan for the administration and coordination of publicly funded student aid in California, Phase I.* Sacramento, Calif.: California State Scholarship and Loan Commission, 1975.

Presents the commission's report and recommendations on the determination of financial need, aid application forms, student aid research, management and staff training, dissemination of information to students, and coordination of aid programs.

VII.E.6. California State Scholarship and Loan Commission. *Student resources survey.* Student Financial Aid Research Series. Report No. 1. Sacramento, Calif.: California State Scholarship and Loan Commission, 1972.

Surveys the personal, academic, and financial characteristics of students attending colleges and universities in the state in 1971–72. Provides an analysis of their expenses, family and personal financial resources, and receipt of aid from various sources by race, type of institution attended, and family income intervals.

VII.E.7. California State Student Aid Commission. *California student resource survey no. 2.* Sacramento, Calif.: California State Student Aid Commission, 1976.

Surveys students at California public and private colleges. Examines their personal, educational, and financial characteristics in the context of assessing their costs of education and their ability to pay those costs.

VII.E.8. California State Student Aid Commission. *Master plan for the administration and coordination of publicly funded student aid in California, Phase II.* Sacramento, Calif.: California State Student Aid Commission, 1977.

Report and recommendation on the second phase of the master plan. Primarily concerned with the coordination of the delivery system of student aid.

VII.E.9. Cogdell, R. T. *The impact of federal student financial assistance on undergraduate students in colleges of the District of Columbia.* Washington: The Catholic University of America, 1971. (Dissertation)

Describes the overall situation in the District of Columbia with regard to the federal NDSL, SEOG, and CWSP programs.

VII.E.10. College Entrance Examination Board. *An analysis of the aggregate financial needs of Kentucky's postsecondary students.* Frankfort, Ky.: Kentucky Higher Education Assistance Authority, 1973.

Estimates the aggregate financial aid needs, resources, and unmet needs of undergraduates enrolled in seven types of postsecondary institutions in the state in 1971–72. Models to forecast the aggregate need under three different sets of conditions are offered.

VII.E.11. College Entrance Examination Board and Brookdale Associates. *A survey of plans for education and careers of Pennsylvania high school seniors, Fall, 1975.* Harrisburg, Pa.: Pennsylvania Higher Education Assistance Agency, 1976.

Surveys the postsecondary plans of nearly 10,000 high school seniors to determine the characteristics of students with educational and vocational plans and the reasons for those plans. Financial aid and college costs were shown to be important factors in the students' choices of postsecondary institutions.

VII.E.12. College Entrance Examination Board and Brookdale Associates. *Student resource survey no. 2.* Harrisburg, Pa.: Pennsylvania Higher Education Assistance Agency, 1975a.

Surveys the personal, academic, and financial characteristics of students enrolled in Pennsylvania postsecondary institutions in 1975–76. Data are analyzed by each of eight types of institutions, including proprietary schools, and compared to findings of an earlier 1972–73 study.

VII.E.13. College Entrance Examination Board and Brookdale Associates. *Undergraduate student financial aid needs and resources in New Jersey colleges and universities, 1973–74.* Princeton, N.J.: New Jersey Commission on Financing Postsecondary Education, 1975b.

Surveys personal, academic, and financial characteristics of full-time undergraduates attending colleges in the state. Special attention is given to their costs of education, resources available to pay for their education, and their need for additional financial aid to reasonably afford these costs.

VII.E.14. Creech, J. D. *Georgia financial aid study.* Atlanta: Southern Regional Office, College Entrance Examination Board, 1972.

Reports on two financial aid studies in the state in 1972: (1) an analysis of the aggregate costs, student and family resources, available financial aid, and unmet need of undergraduates enrolled in postsecondary education, and (2) a survey of the postsecondary plans of 5,000 high school seniors.

VII.E.15. Davis, J. S. *A report on undergraduate student financial aid needs and resources in New Jersey colleges and universities, 1973–74.* Trenton, N.J.: New Jersey State Department of Higher Education, 1975.

Studies the aggregate financial aid needs, resources, and unmet needs of full-time undergraduates. Data are analyzed by family income levels within different institutional types.

VII.E.16. Davis, J. S. *Student financial aid needs and resources in the* SREB *states: A comparative analysis.* Atlanta: Southern Regional Education Board, 1974.

Studies the aggregate costs, financial aid needs, available resources, and unmet needs of students attending postsecondary institutions in 14 Southern states in 1971–72. State and regional data are compared by institutional types and family income characteristics of students.

VII.E.17. Davis, J. S. and Van Dusen, W. D. *Who needs what? A study of the financial needs and resources of full-time undergraduate students in the state of Iowa, 1974–75.* Des Moines, Iowa: Higher Education Facilities Commission of the State of Iowa, 1975.

Examines the aggregate needs, available resources, and need for additional aid of full-time undergraduates. Data are analyzed by institutional types, student family income intervals, and in-state and out-of-state student residency statuses.

VII.E.18. Dent, R. A., Blair, S. J., and Nelson, J. E. *Student financing of higher education in Washington: An analysis of the resources used by students in paying for their college educations.* Palo Alto, Calif.: Western Regional Office, College Entrance Examination Board, 1972.

Reports on a 1971–72 survey of over 27,000 students enrolled in public and private two-year and four-year colleges in Washington. Describes the personal, academic, family, and financial characteristics of students, paying particular attention to the role of financial aid in paying for educational costs.

VII.E.19. Dent, D., Cutler, N., Westine, J., and Stearns, F. *Oregon student resource survey.* Salem, Ore.: Educational Coordinating Council, 1973.

Reports on a survey of over 32,000 Oregon students enrolled in 39 colleges and universities and ten proprietary institutions in 1972–73. Analyzes personal, academic, family, and financial characteristics of students at each type of institution, directing special attention to the ways in which financial aid was distributed among all students.

VII.E.20. Donovan, C. *An historical summary of financial aid provided students in Washington, 1972–73 through 1976–77.* Olympia, Wash.: Council for Postsecondary Education, 1977a.

Contains a capsulized summary of financial aid available to students in public and private postsecondary institutions in Washington. Includes data on federal, state, and institutional programs.

VII.E.21. Donovan, C. *An overview of the spring term 1976 survey of student resources and financing patterns.* Olympia, Wash.: Council for Postsecondary Education, 1977b.

Summarizes the results of a student resource survey of students enrolled at public and private colleges and proprietary schools in Washington. Describes the students' racial-ethnic, marital, and dependency statuses, then family incomes, employment, financial resources, and costs by various segments of institutional types.

VII. E. 22. Erbschloe, R. R. *Financial aid programs in Arizona postsecondary educational institutions.* Tempe, Ariz.: Arizona State University, 1976. (Dissertation)

Studies the management, administration, and distribution of financial aid resources at Arizona institutions from 1972-73 through 1974-75.

VII. E. 23. Educational Management Services, Inc. *Model student assistance programs for Kentucky.* Frankfort, Ky.: Kentucky Higher Education Assistance Authority, 1973.

Describes model student assistance programs for the state. Considers financial aid program goals, administrative procedures, program guidelines, and funding levels and methods as essential elements in the models.

VII. E. 24. Fife, J. D. *A report on the status of higher education student financial aid in Maryland.* Annapolis, Md.: Governor's Study Commission on Structure and Governance of Education, 1975.

Reviews the status of financial aid in relation to equal access to postsecondary education, changing demands for education, attendance, trends in the growth of higher education, the students' ability to pay for education, and the interaction of state, federal, and institutional aid programs.

VII. E. 25. Glover, R. E. and Chapman, B. *A report on student aid needs within the postsecondary education community in Arkansas.* Little Rock, Ark.: Arkansas State Postsecondary Education Planning Commission, 1975.

Analyzes the financial aid needs of students at colleges and universities, vocation-technical schools, and proprietary schools in 1973-74. Projects future aid needs and recommends ways to meet them.

VII. E. 26. Governor's Task Force on Financing Higher Education. *Higher education in New York State.* Albany, N.Y.: Governor's Task Force, 1973.

Reports and recommendations of the task force. Major findings concern postsecondary education finance and capital, enrollments, financial aid, diversity, quality, governance, and future manpower requirements.

VII. E. 27. Haberaelker, H. J. and Wagner, R. D. *Student access, scholarship, and loan programs: Report of the study committee on tuition and other student costs for master plan phase IV.* Springfield, Ill.: Illinois State Board of Higher Education, 1975.

Reviews present tuition and financial aid policies, then recommends specific changes in policies and discusses their implications for student access and choice.

VII. E. 28. Iowa State Higher Education Facilities Commission. *Post high school plans and financial needs of Iowa students.* Iowa State Higher Education Facilities Commission, 1975.

Summarizes two 1974-75 statewide studies: one of the postsecondary plans of Iowa high school seniors and another of the financial aid needs and resources of Iowa undergraduates. Includes statistical data and tables.

VII. E. 29. Kentucky Higher Education Assistance Agency. *A survey of student financial aid resources in Kentucky, July, 1973.* Frankfort, Ky.: Kentucky Higher Education Assistance Agency, 1973.

Studies financial aid resources available to students at public and private colleges and universities, vocational-technical schools, business colleges, Bible colleges, and state-approved proprietary schools in 1972–73.

VII. E. 30. Montana State Commissioner of Higher Education. *A study of the accessibility of the postsecondary institutions of Montana.* Helena, Mont.: Board of Regents for Higher Education, 1976.

Reports on availability of postsecondary education to residents of the state.

VII. E. 31. New Jersey Commission on Financing Postsecondary Education. *Family financial circumstances and patterns of financing a college education.* Princeton, N.J.: New Jersey Commission on Financing Postsecondary Education, 1975.

Analyzes the financial resources and aid available to students from different family income intervals who were full-time undergraduates at New Jersey colleges and universities in 1973–74.

VII. E. 32. New Jersey Commission on Financing Postsecondary Education. *Student resource survey of selected New Jersey residents attending college in another state.* Princeton, N.J.: New Jersey Commission on Financing Postsecondary Education, 1976.

Surveys the personal, academic, and financial characteristics of New Jersey residents enrolled as sophomores in out-of-state colleges in 1974–75. Analyzed their reasons for attending their institutions and their plans for returning to the state after graduation.

VII. E. 33. New York State Board of Regents. *Financial aid for New York students. A report to the governor and the legislature in fulfillment of Section 606 of the Education Law.* Albany, N.Y.: New York State Education Department, 1974.

Reviews current state programs; studies characteristics of award recipients and how they finance their education.

VII. E. 34. Pennsylvania Higher Education Assistance Agency. *A study of the characteristics and resources of students in postsecondary education in the Commonwealth of Pennsylvania.* Harrisburg, Pa.: Pennsylvania Higher Education Assistance Agency, 1975.

Studies the personal, academic, and financial characteristics of students enrolled in Pennsylvania postsecondary institutions in 1972–73. Data are analyzed by students' racial-ethnic background and types of institutions attended.

VII. E. 35. State of Florida Department of Education. *Student financial assistance in Florida: Final report, February, 1976.* Tallahassee, Fla.: State of Florida Department of Education, 1976.

Reports on the financial aid needs of students in Florida postsecondary institutions, on the role of state and federal aid in financing student costs, and on the administration of state, federal, and institutional aid programs.

VII.E.36. University of Delaware, Division of Urban Affairs. *Estimates of financial aid requirements for Delaware's postsecondary students.* Newark, Del.: Division of Urban Affairs, University of Delaware, 1975.

A report to the Postsecondary Education Commission on the financial aid resources available to Delaware's postsecondary students. Estimates future aid requirements.

VII.E.37. Van Dusen, W. D. *Student needs and resources in Montana postsecondary education.* Helena, Mont.: Montana Commission on Postsecondary Education, 1974.

Surveys more than 10,000 full-time students enrolled in Montana public institutions in the 1973-74 academic year. Provides information about their personal, social, and academic characteristics; and their expenses, resources, and methods of financing postsecondary education. Includes comparisons indicating that student-reported parental income data closely corresponds to that available from external sources.

VII.E.38. Van Dusen, W. D. and Davis, J. S. *The matter of choice: A study of the use of grants administered by the Pennsylvania Higher Education Assistance Agency by students attending institutions in another state.* Harrisburg, Pa.: Pennsylvania Higher Education Assistance Agency, 1975.

Studies the personal and academic characteristics, educational expenses, family financial resources, and financial aid resources of students who used PHEAA awards at out-of-state postsecondary institutions in 1974. Considers why students leave the state for educational purposes and what they might do if state aid was not available to support them.

VII.E.39. Vermont Higher Education Planning Commission. *Financing access to postsecondary education in Vermont.* Burlington, Vt.: Vermont Higher Education Planning Commission, 1976.

Examines the financial barriers to postsecondary education and the costs of removing them.

VII.E.40. Virginia State Council of Higher Education. *An analysis of student financial aid and state aid to private higher education in Virginia.* Richmond, Va.: Virginia State Council of Higher Education, 1975.

Reports on two studies: (1) the financial plight of private colleges in Virginia and form of aid to them and their students and (2) the aggregate costs, family and student resources, available aid, and unmet needs of undergraduates at all public and private colleges in the state.

VII.E.41. West Virginia Board of Regents. *Financial aid resources available to students attending West Virginia colleges and universities.* Charleston, W. Va.: West Virginia Board of Regents, 1974.

Studies the total aid resources directed to students at West Virginia colleges in

1973-74 and estimates the resources available for 1974-75. Data includes aid to full-time and part-time students and to in-state and out-of-state students.

VII.F. Studies Concerning Special Student Groups

The references in this section describe research on special student groups, including health professions students, graduate and professional school students, minority students, community college students, female students, transfer students, part-time students, married students, foreign students, independent students, and students in attendance at specific postsecondary institutions. The items cited are concerned with student characteristics and patterns of financing and with the administration of programs designed to meet their special needs.

Seven of the following documents discuss student financing in health professions programs. Crocker (1974) and Lambdin (1975) report on the financial resources and expenses of medical school students in 1971 and 1974 respectively. Bowman (1974) describes the results of a national survey of institutions participating in federal Health Professions Student Loan and Scholarship Programs. The National Academy of Sciences (1973) studies the federal support of researchers in biomedical science. Schueller and McKenna (1973) analyze characteristics of dental research graduate trainees and fellows, and Feldstein (1974) presents an evaluation of federal support of dental education. The Academy for Educational Development (1976) reports on the financing of students and colleges of podiatric medicine.

A National Science Foundation (1970) study describes the characteristics and financial support of 146,000 graduate students enrolled in science curriculums. A more recent study of this same population includes trend-line data on changes in their financial patterns between 1967 and 1973 (Foster, et al., 1975). Baggett and Jones (1974) study the financial aid status of graduate students who are receiving veterans benefits to attend a public college. They find that the benefits would not pay for the students' cost of education. Hochman and Nietfeld (1976) study sources of financing for male and female graduate students at Michigan State University and conclude that no sex discrimination existed in the distribution of student aid resources. Rodgers (1972) describes alternative aid programs to meet the financial needs of professional school students.

Minority students are the subject of five studies. Watley (1971) analyzes data on students who took the National Merit Scholarship Qualifying Test to compare financial patterns of black and nonblack students. A statewide study of the operation and impact of New Jersey's Educational Opportunity Program (EOP) is presented by the State Legislature's Office of Fiscal Affairs (1973). The EOP is a special state student aid program that provides financial aid and other support services to minority/poverty students in New Jersey colleges.

Hayes (1975) finds that black students at Michigan State University received less parental support and more support from aid programs than white students. Chicano Economic Opportunity Program award recipients at a California college were the subject of research by Immenhausen (1975), who reveals that their grades were lower than those of other EOP students.

A study of the financial aid needs and resources of students at predominantly black private colleges is reported by the College Entrance Examination Board and Brookdale Associates (1976). This study employs the Student Resource Survey and compares the results with SRS data from students at predominantly white private colleges.

Financial aid to community college students is the subject of three items. Gladieux (1975) reports on the distribution of federal student aid to these students, and concludes that they receive proportionately fewer dollars than their needs warrant. Garcea (1975) reports on the resources and expenditures of students at three community colleges in the Northwest; Blocker and Snyder (1971) study the effects of student aid packaging on persistence and achievement at five community colleges in Pennsylvania.

Financial aid to women is the topic of three studies. Cox and Van Dusen (1969) and Froomkin (1974) discuss the ways in which educational borrowing affect the financing of women's education. The former study found that, in 1968, over 80 percent of the women borrowers believed that borrowing was a good experience. The latter report indicates that current loan repayment plans make debt financing for educational purposes less attractive to women than to men. Eckhoudt (1976) describes the financial aid status of women at the University of Washington.

Breuder (1972) compares the financial aid awards received by new freshmen and by transfer students at Florida State University and finds that both groups received equal amounts of aid. However, Van Dusen (1974) uses Student Resource Service data from four states to show that first-time students were more likely than transfer students to receive aid and that the latter group had to make up greater percentages of their resources from outside employment.

Three studies of the financial needs and resources of part-time students indicate that their aid needs are substantial and typically unmet by current aid programs. Mangham (1975) reports that aid policies at California community colleges inhibited part-time student enrollment. English's (1974) survey of part-time students at nine colleges in Illinois indicates that students attended on a part-time basis due to financial reasons. Brici (1972) finds that part-time students supported their education through employment rather than financial aid or other family resources.

Four studies describe the financial need and aid situations of students at individual colleges (Kane, 1970; Rist, 1970; Schonhart, 1977; Trombley, 1975). A fifth study concerns the distribution and impact of financial aid on students at private colleges in the Midwest (Rauh, 1972).

Two ACT Research Reports provide important data on the impact of financial need and aid. The first is a study of student migration patterns of college attendance (Fenske, et al., 1972). This report indicates that there is a trend toward less interstate and intrastate migration to attend colleges. The second report describes the impact of financial need on student vocational decision-making. Vanderwell (1970) reports that students whose needs were fully met were more likely than others to have made firmer choices about majors and vocational goals.

Bergen, et al. (1977) describe the resources and expenditures of married students at a midwestern university. Stecklein and Liv (1974) report on a 1974 survey of foreign students' financial aid needs and resources. Nelson, et al. (1974) use a national data base to test the financial implications of alternative definitions of independent student status for financial aid purposes. Lidstrom (1975) describes the characteristics of selected community college students who received corporate tuition reimbursements to attend school.

Five items provide helpful data bases for research and inquiry in financial aid. Four are U.S. Bureau of the Census (1972a, 1972b, 1974, 1975) reports describing financial and other demographic characteristics of students in postsecondary education. The fifth is a research report by Horch (1973) that describes the demographic and economic characteristics of over 800,000 families whose dependents applied for financial aid at some institution.

VII.F.1. Academy for Educational Development. *A deferred cost of education plan for podiatric medicine*. Washington, D.C.: American Association of Colleges of Podiatric Medicine, 1976.

Reports on the financial needs and prospects of students and colleges of podiatric medicine; develops a new plan for the financing of podiatric medicine.

VII.F.2. Baggett, W. and Jones, B. The sources of financial aid of graduate students with veterans status at one university. *Journal of Student Financial Aid*, Vol. 4, November 1974, pp. 36–40.

Survey of 323 graduate students receiving VA benefits at Southern Illinois University. Reveals they had difficulty in meeting costs on current-level payments.

VII.F.3. Bergen, G. R., Bergen, M. B., and Meisner, R. Financial needs of married students: Whose responsibility? *Journal of Student Financial Aid,* Vol. 7, May 1977, pp. 5–9.

Survey of the sources and amounts of resources and types and amounts of expenditures of 327 married student couples at a midwestern university in 1976. Found that married student expenditures exceeded financial aid administrators' expected budgets. Discuss implications for policymakers.

VII. F.4. Blocker, C. E. and Snyder, F. A. *Financial aids for community college students.* Harrisburg, Pa.: Harrisburg Area Community College, 1971.

Study of the effects of student aid packaging on student persistence and achievement at five community colleges in Pennsylvania.

VII.F.5. Bowman, J. L. *Measuring student financial need in health profession student loan and scholarship programs.* Washington, D.C.: Bureau of Health Manpower, Public Service, Department of Health, Education, and Welfare, 1974.

Results of a national survey of institutional participants in the federal Health Professions Student Loan and Scholarship programs. The survey is used to describe institutional practices in need analysis and in administration of the programs.

VII.F.6. Breuder, R. L. A study of the distribution of financial aid awarded by Florida State University to Florida public junior college transfer students and incoming freshmen. *Journal of Student Financial Aid,* Vol. 2, May 1972, pp. 23–31.

Analyzes data for fall 1970 to show that community college transfer students and beginning freshmen received equal amounts of aid from the university. Discusses the case for increasing the proportion of institutionalized aid monies to transfer students.

VII.F.7. Brici, M. S. *A study of financial support sources utilized by part- and full-time students enrolled in associate degree programs.* Bloomington, Ind.: Indiana University, 1972. (Dissertation)

Compares six demographic and 13 financial characteristics of 389 students at two colleges in spring 1971. Finds that part-time students utilize fewer support sources (primarily their own wages and earnings) than full-time students.

VII.F.8. College Entrance Examination Board and Brookdale Associates. *The ways and means: A study of the needs and resources of students enrolled in United Negro College Fund member institutions.* New York: United Negro College Fund, 1976. (Mimeographed)

Surveys students at UNCF colleges in 1975–76. Reports on their personal characteristics, academic goals, and family and financial aid resources. Compares the distribution of resources at these institutions to those at private, predominantly white colleges. Discusses the role of financial aid in institutional finance and the implications of various federal financing proposals.

VII. F. 9. Cox, M. B. and Van Dusen, W. D. How educational borrowing affects the female student. *College Board Review,* No. 71, Spring 1969, pp. 28–31.

Analyzes data from a 1968 survey of Barnard College alumnae on the affects of loans on female students. The survey reveals that: borrowing had little effect on graduate study plans or activities; less than four percent felt they borrowed too much as undergraduates; less than six percent had delayed marriage or childbearing because of indebtedness; less than twelve percent said they had to live at a reduced standard of living because of indebtedness; and more than eight out of ten women believed their borrowing experiences were good ones.

VII. F. 10. Crocker, A. R. *How medical students finance their education.* Bethesda, Md.: Health Resources Administration, Department of Health, Education and Welfare, 1974.

Reports on patterns of expenses and sources of income for students in the health professions in 1971. Includes data on 22,000 students at public and private institutions.

VII. F. 11. Dunning, B. B. and Unger, J. L. *Schools' responses to vouchered vocational training: Experiences with the Portland WIN voucher training program.* Washington, D.C.: Bureau of Social Science Research, Inc., 1975.

Surveys 27 vocational schools in which Work Incentive Program registrants were enrolled during a voucher feasibility test. Reports that the system presented no serious problems for the schools and that neither the students nor the program were being exploited.

VII. F. 12. Eckhoudt, J. *Status of women report.* Seattle: University of Washington, Educational Assessment Center, 1976.

Analysis of admissions, academic performance, financial aid, and student employment of women at the University of Washington. Includes data on graduate and undergraduate students.

VII. F. 13. English, R. J. *Financial need and other characteristics of the part-time undergraduate student in selected colleges and universities in Illinois.* Dekalb, Ill.: Northern Illinois University, 1974. (Dissertation)

Surveys the personal and financial characteristics of 1,008 part-time students in nine colleges. Finds that students attended on a part-time basis for financial reasons, and that part-time students had a proportionately greater need for assistance than full-time students.

VII. F. 14. Feldstein, P. J. *A preliminary evaluation of federal dental manpower subsidy program.* Health Manpower Policy Discussion Paper Series, No. A5. Ann Arbor, Mich.: Michigan University, 1974.

Analyzes the impact of federal manpower programs on dentistry. Suggests an approach to evaluation of manpower policies.

VII. F. 15. Fenske, R. H., Scott, C. S., and Carmody, J. F. *College student migration.* ACT Research Report No. 54. Iowa City, Iowa: American College Testing Program, 1972.

Examines the characteristics of first-time enrolled freshmen attending local colleges, colleges in their home state, in adjacent states, and a distant state in 1966 and 1967. Found more students attended local institutions in the more recent year, regardless of family incomes.

VII. F. 16. Foster, P., et al. *Graduate science education: Student support and postdoctorals, Fall 1973.* Surveys of Science Resources Series No. NSF-74-318. Washington: National Science Foundation, 1975.

Continues survey begun in 1972 to provide national data on financial aid to graduate science and engineering students. Based on responses of 6,559 masters and doctoral departments in 339 institutions. Includes trend-line data from 1967 to 1973.

VII. F. 17. Froomkin, J. *Study of the advantages and disadvantages of student loans to women.* Springfield, Va.: National Technical Information Service, 1974.

Examines the suitability of existing loan arrangements for financing the education of women and evaluates alternative loan repayment rules and arrangements that would make debt financing correspond to women's earning patterns.

VII. F. 18. Garcea, R. A. *Spending and financial patterns of community college students.* Pullman, Wash.: Washington State University, 1975. (Dissertation)

Surveys 1,019 students at three community colleges to determine their sources of financial resources and types of educational expenditures. The colleges were in three geographically different areas. No differences in resources by colleges were found. However, students at the large urban college had to spend more on living, transportation, and personal expenses.

VII. F. 19. Gladieux, L. E. *Distribution of federal student assistance: The enigma of the two-year college.* New York: College Entrance Examination Board, 1975.

Reports on the distribution of federal student aid to community college students across the nation. Offers several reasons for their underparticipation in federal programs. Indicates that a fully funded BEOG program would deliver more aid to community college students than is currently received through campus-based programs.

VII. F. 20. Hayes, A. G. A study of economic needs of selected black and white students at a northern university. *Journal of Student Financial Aid,* Vol. 5, March 1975, pp. 4–16.

Reports on a survey of black students at Michigan State University. Shows that, compared to white students, black students received less support from their families and more support from aid programs; they needed more money management counseling; and they had fewer funds to meet personal needs.

VII. F. 21. Hochman, L. M. and Nietfeld, C. R. Differences in sources of financing of female and male Michigan State University graduate students. *Journal of College Student Personnel*, Vol. 17, January 1976, pp. 55–60.

Reports on a 1973 survey of 248 students which reveals little evidence of sex discrimination in sources of financing but does indicate significant differences in education choices that affect income sources.

VII. F. 22. Holmstrom, E. I. *Low income students: Do they differ from "typical" undergraduates?* ACE Research Reports Vol. 8, No. 5, 1973.

Uses survey data collected in 1967 and 1971 to compare the academic, personal, and family characteristics and graduation rates of typical and low-income undergraduates. Found that low-income students had similar aspirations, life goals, and patterns of college activities and studies. Low-income students were less likely than other students to graduate in four years if they attended highly selective institutions. Low-income students tended to rely more on parents for financial support as they progressed through college.

VII. F. 23. Horch, D. H. *A description of families who filed 1971–72 and 1972–73 Parents' Confidential Statements with the College Scholarship Service.* Princeton, N.J.: College Scholarship Service, 1973.

Analyzes the demographic and economic characteristics of over 800,000 families whose dependents had applied for aid at some college or university. Describes their occupational statuses, incomes, sources of income, expenses and indebtedness, and assets.

VII. F. 24. Immenhausen, R. L. Academic performance of Chicano EOG recipients. *Journal of Student Financial Aid*, Vol. 5, March 1975, pp. 50–56.

Compares the performance of 32 matched pairs of Chicano and other students in the EOP program at College of the Desert (California). Reveals no significant differences in the ability to predict their grades from ACT scores. Chicano students' mean grade-point averages were lower than those of other students.

VII. F. 25. Kane, J. G. *A comparative study of academic success and other selected characteristics of financial aid and non-financial aid recipients at Winona State College.* Corvallis, Ore.: Oregon State University, 1970. (Dissertation)

Compares personal attitudes and perceptions, educational and vocational plans, and satisfaction of over- and under-achieving aid recipients and nonrecipients. Students who received aid performed better than those not receiving aid.

VII. F. 26. Lambdin, J. A. *Survey of how medical students finance their education.* Washington, D.C.: Association of American Medical Colleges, 1975.

Reports on survey of medical students in 1974–75. Describes how they finance their education and how these patterns compare with data obtained for 1968 and 1971. Data include student characteristics, average annual expenses, and sources of income.

VII.F.27. Lidstrom, K. *An investigation of the number of students receiving corporate tuition reimbursement in eleven sections of Introduction to Business 460-108 at Cuyahoga Community College.* Fort Lauderdale, Fla.: Nova University, 1975. (Practicum)

Studies characteristics of students receiving corporate tuition reimbursements for educational costs. Describes the types and amounts of payments received and suggests a plan for attracting such students to increase college enrollments and income.

VII.F.28. Mangham, C. *Part-time students.* Sacramento, Calif.: Board of Governors of the California Community Colleges, 1975.

Reviews the extent to which fee structures, admission policies, and financial aid policies at California community colleges inhibit or enhance access of part-time students. Suggests that financial constraints often limit the extent to which part-time students can be served.

VII.F.29. National Academy of Sciences, National Research Council. *Postdoctoral training in the biomedical sciences: An evaluation of National Institute of General Medical Sciences postdoctoral traineeship and fellowship programs.* Washington, D.C.: National Technical Information Service, 1973.

Study of the history and effectivness of NIGMS programs in support of training researchers in biomedical research.

VII.F.30. National Science Foundation. *Graduate student support and manpower resources in graduate science education.* Washington, D.C.: Government Printing Office, 1970.

Report on enrollment and staffing in graduate science programs. Describes the characteristics and financial support of 146,000 graduate students.

VII.F.31. Nelson, J. E., Rice, L. D., Jacobson, E. C., and Van Dusen, W. D. *Who is the independent student? A study of the status and resources of independent students.* New York: College Entrance Examination Board, 1974.

Uses a data base collected by the College Entrance Examination Board to test alternative definitions of independent students. Describes the financial aid implications of each definition. Concludes that policy restrictions on the distribution of grant awards to independent students would not increase the equitable distribution of aid funds.

VII.F.32. Office of Fiscal Affairs. *Program analysis of the New Jersey Educational Opportunity Fund.* Trenton, N.J.: New Jersey State Legislature, 1973.

Reports on the development, operation, and impact of the state's financial aid program for minority/poverty students.

VII.F.33. Rauh, M. A. *Student financial aid at private colleges: A study of the twenty-four colleges comprising the Associated Colleges of the Midwest and Great Lakes Colleges Association.* Yellow Springs, Ohio: Morton A. Ruah, 1972.

Investigates the distribution of financial aid at private, midwestern colleges and its relationship to institutional finances.

VII. F. 34. Rist, M. G. *A study of freshman financial aid awards with respect to student need.* Ann Arbor, Mich.: Michigan State University, 1970. (Dissertation)

Studies aid awards made to 170 freshmen at the University of South Dakota to determine if the needs of various student groups were fulfilled in the same manner by grants and self-help.

VII. F. 35. Rodgers, G. McC. *Student financial aid in professional schools: An analysis of policy alternatives.* Palo Alto, Calif.: Stanford University, 1972. (Dissertation)

Investigates programs designed to meet the aid needs of professional school students. Concludes that financial needs can be feasibly met by a fixed-obligation loan program drawing on funds from outside the institution.

VII. F. 36. Schonhart, P. T. No need freshmen: How were educational costs met? *Journal of Student Financial Aid,* Vol. 7, February 1977, pp. 50–55.

Surveys the financial resources of 357 freshmen who were denied aid by the State University of New York College at Fredonia. Over 55 percent of their resources came from parents, 10 percent from summer savings and part-time jobs, and the remainder from state grant programs, the GSLP, or other aid sources. On the average, parents contributed only 42 percent of the amounts expected under need analysis.

VII. F. 37. Schueller, G. K. and McKenna, T. W. *Follow-up survey of National Institute of Dental Research graduate trainees and postdoctoral fellows.* Rockville, Md.: Westat Research, Inc., 1973.

Reports on 1,822 trainees and fellows who received NIDR support. Describes their demographic characteristics and training and employment experiences. Presents data on their attitudes about the program.

VII. F. 38. Stancil, W. J. *Vietnam era G.I. benefits: A Michigan tri-county survey on advance payment and work-study.* Warren, Mich.: Macomb County Community College, 1973.

Examines the responses of 36 institutions to the Veterans Administration advance payment and work-study programs.

VII. F. 39. Stecklein, J. E. and Liv, H. C. *Study of foreign student employment and financial resources. Part I: Institutional survey. Part II: Individual survey.* Washington, D.C.: National Association for Foreign Student Affairs, 1974.

Reports on a 1974 survey of 52 colleges with the largest foreign student enrollments and a survey of foreign students at one private and six public institutions. Includes data on visa status, sex, marital and dependent status, employment activities and needs, and financial resources and needs.

VII.F.40. Trombley, P. W. *A study of undergraduate student financial need at Western Michigan University for the 1974–75 academic year*. Kalamazoo, Mich.: Western Michigan University, 1975. (Dissertation)

Interviews with 109 students reveal that both aid recipients and nonrecipients had more income resources than expenditures.

VII.F.41. U.S. Bureau of the Census. *School enrollment – Social and economic characteristics of students: October, 1974*. Current Population Reports, Series P-20, No. 286, 1975.

Contains detailed information on elementary, secondary, and postsecondary enrollments by sex, race, age, family income, marital status, and residence. Data are not described for states.

VII.F.42. U.S. Bureau of the Census. *Social and economic characteristics of students: October, 1971*. Current Population Reports, Series P-20, No. 241, 1972a.

Contains detailed information on elementary, secondary, and postsecondary enrollments by sex, race, age, family income, marital status, and residence. Data are not described for states.

VII.F.43. U.S. Bureau of the Census. *Social and economic characteristics of students: October, 1973*. Current Population Reports, Series P-20, No. 272, 1974.

Contains detailed information on elementary, secondary, and postsecondary enrollments by sex, age, family income, marital status, and residence.

VII.F.44. U.S. Bureau of the Census. *Undergraduate enrollment in two-year and four-year colleges: October, 1971*. Current Population Reports, Series P-20, No. 236, 1972b.

Contains data on enrollments by sex, race, age, family income, marital status, and residence. Data are not described for states.

VII.F.45. Vanderwell, A. R. *Influence of financial need on the vocational development of college students*. ACT Research Reports No. 36, 1970.

Examines the impact of financial need on the vocational decision-making of 291 second-semester students at four public colleges. Students whose financial aid needs were fully met were more likely than those not receiving sufficient aid or the nonapplicants to have made firmer choices about majors and vocational goals.

VII.F.46. Van Dusen, W. D. A forgotten minority: The transfer student needs financial aid too. *College Board Review*, No. 92, Summer 1974, pp. 17–20.

Analysis of data from four statewide student resource surveys in 1971–72 reveals that first-time students were slightly more likely than transfer students to receive financial aid but the percentages of total support received by both groups from parents/spouse, savings, and borrowing were comparable. Due to reduced availability of grants and CWSP earnings, transfer students had to make up greater percentages of resources from outside employment.

VII.F.47. Watley, D. J. *Black and nonblack youth: Finances and college attendance.* Evanston, Ill.: National Merit Scholarship Corp., 1971.

Surveys 28,800 National Merit Scholarship Qualifying Test participants to determine what financial resources they used to pay for college. Data are analyzed on the basis of race, sex, ability levels, and geographic region of residence.

VII.F.48. Wise, M., et al. Fellowships in medical education. *Journal of Medical Education,* Vol. 49, February 1974, pp. 146–153.

Studies recipients of health professions' fellowships to determine their motivation for seeking training, their responsibilities after training, and evidence of consequent educational leadership. Results reveal a shift in medical education from teaching and research to administration.

VII.G. Tuition and Student Expenses

Many of the items cited here represent surveys of student expense budgets as estimated by aid administrators. They include two studies by the United States Office of Education (Podolsky, 1975, 1976), a report on an annual survey by the College Scholarship Service (Suchar, et al., 1976), and a research report on student aid budgets at colleges in the Southwest (Ferrin, 1971). A fifth item uses data from a variety of publications to relate student costs to ability to pay (Harris, 1972).

The major value of these surveys is that they permit comparisons of cost trends among institutions over time. They also permit analysis of similarities and differences in types and amounts of charges and costs to students. The major disadvantage of the data is that they may not be valid; that is, the aid administrator estimates of nonfixed charges may not represent the expenses students really incur. As indicated in the statewide studies described in Section VII.E, aid administrator and student estimates of educational expenses are often significantly different. Van Dusen, et al. (1974) also find inconsistencies in student reports of educational costs and estimated budgets used by aid administrators and the Basic Educational Opportunity Grants Program.

It is, of course, possible that *student* reports on expenditures are not valid. Bowman (1975) examines some of the problems of collecting valid data on student expenses from students and other sources. Wagner (1976) also discusses the issues of budget construction and attendant validity questions.

Two student surveys of educational expenses are cited below. One is a United States Bureau of the Census (1975) report on income and expenses of students in postsecondary institutions in October 1973. Another is a report on the expenditure patterns of 2,200 students who used the

American College Testing Program's Need Analysis Service in 1972. One important and unique feature of this latter study is that it describes the extent to which students make contributions to parents, rather than vice versa (Jepsen, 1973).

Halstead (1975, 1976) uses data from several sources to establish price indexes in higher education from 1961 to 1975 for several items, including student consumer prices. His research indicates that students paid twice as much in 1974 as they did in 1961 for the same real resources expended by institutions.

The real costs of education to students have not yet been determined to everyone's satisfaction. The evidence considered in the studies cited below indicates that student costs have increased annually during the 1970s and that this trend will continue into the next decade. However, true and accurate data on student costs have not yet been assembled for any given group of students; only approximate cost estimates exist.

In view of the apparent (and probably real) need for increased financial aid to meet higher costs, and the attention given to plans in which students will pay for more of the total education bill, there is a significant need for more accurate data on the real costs of educational experiences.

VII.G.1. Bowman, W. W. *Estimating the costs of college students.* Berkeley, Calif.: The Chancellor's Management Analysis Group, University of California, 1975. (Mimeographed)

Reports on the use of student diaries, interviews, and other techniques to determine student maintenance budgets.

VII.G.2. Ferrin, R. I. *Student budgets and aid awarded in southwestern colleges.* Higher Education Surveys Report No. 5. New York: College Entrance Examination Board, 1971.

Analyzes student budgets and aid available to meet them at southwestern colleges and universities in 1970–71 and 1971–72. Based on a survey of campus aid administrators, the report concludes that aid met only 16 percent of private college expenses, 10 percent of public four-year college expenses, and less than 8 percent of community college expenses.

VII.G.3. Halstead, D. K. *Higher education prices and price indexes.* Washington, D.C.; Government Printing Office, 1975.

Using data from a variety of sources, analyzes price trends in current operations, research and development, physical plant additions, and student consumer prices. Shows that students paid about twice as much in 1974 as they did in 1961 for the same real resources expended by institutions

VII.G.4. Halstead, D. K. *Higher education prices and price indexes: 1975 supplement.* Washington, D.C.: Government Printing Office, 1976.

Revises prices and price indexes of earlier publication to include 1975 data on expenditures by and for higher education since 1971.

VII.G.5. Harris, S. E. Student expenses. In *A statistical portrait of higher education*. New York: McGraw-Hill, 1972.

Presents tables on student costs and ability to pay, graduate student expenses, and sources of funds. Most data are for years prior to 1967.

VII.G.6. Jepsen, K. J., Maxey, E. J., and Henry, J. B. Student expenditure patterns. *Journal of Student Financial Aid*, Vol. 3, November 1973, pp. 3-9.

Describes the expenditure patterns of 2,200 students who used the ACT need analysis service in 1972, comparing their self-help contributions to expectations and discussing the extent of student contributions to parents rather than vice versa.

VII.G.7. Podolsky, A. *Basic student charges, 1972-73 and 1973-74*. Washington, D.C.: National Center for Education Statistics, 1975.

Contains data on tuition and fees and room and board expenses for undergraduate and graduate students at public and private colleges and universities.

VII.G.8. Podolsky, A. *Basic student charges, academic year 1974-75, higher education*. Washington, D.C.: Government Printing Office, 1976.

Contains data on costs of tuition and fees and room and board for undergraduate and graduate students at individual colleges across the nation. Compares aggregate average costs by institutional types for 1972-73, 1973-74, and 1974-75.

VII.G.9. Sonnenberg, W. C. Financial sources for postsecondary students. *American Education*, Vol. 11, November 1975. (Back cover)

One-page summary of data contained in the Bureau of the Census publication, *Income and Expenses of Students Enrolled in Postsecondary Schools, October, 1973*.

VII.G.10. Suchar, E. W., Ivens, S., and Jacobson, E. C. *Student expenses at postsecondary institutions, 1976-77*. New York: College Entrance Examination Board, 1976. (Title published annually since 1973)

Contains data on average student budgets at more than 2,500 postsecondary institutions. Compares growth in expenses over the preceding years by types of expenditures and institutions.

VII.G.11. U.S. Bureau of the Census. *Income and expenses of students enrolled in postsecondary schools: October, 1973*. Current Population Reports, Series P-20, No. 281, 1975.

Reports on the income and expenses of postsecondary students in 1973. Data are analyzed by sex, race, full-time and part-time attendance status, marital status, financial dependence on parents, and types of institutions attended.

VII.G.12. Van Dusen, W. D., Jacobson, E. C., and Wagner, A. P. *Analyses of student costs of attendance.* Washington, D.C.: Washington Office, College Entrance Examination Board, 1974. (Mimeographed)

Using national data summaries, compares institutional guidance budgets, need analysis budgets, and BEOG Program budgets for consistency and inconsistency.

VII.G.13. Wagner, A. P. *Cutting the coat to fit the cloth: Student expense budgets.* Washington, D.C.: Washington Office, College Entrance Examination Board, 1976. (Mimeographed)

Discusses several broad issues in budget construction and evaluates different methods for collecting student expense data.